The
WILDFLOWER
BOOK

FROM THE ROCKIES WEST

Indeed, are they not all riddles? Where is the flower which even to the most devoted of us has yet confided all of its mysteries?
WILLIAM HAMILTON GIBSON, *Eye Spy*, 1897

STOKES NATURE GUIDES

BY DONALD STOKES

A Guide to Nature in Winter
A Guide to Observing Insect Lives
A Guide to Bird Behavior, Volume I

BY DONALD AND LILLIAN STOKES

A Guide to Bird Behavior, Volume II
A Guide to Bird Behavior, Volume III
A Guide to Enjoying Wildflowers
A Guide to Animal Tracking and Behavior

BY THOMAS F. TYNING

A Guide to Amphibians and Reptiles

STOKES BACKYARD NATURE BOOKS

BY DONALD AND LILLIAN STOKES

The Bird Feeder Book
The Hummingbird Book
The Complete Birdhouse Book
The Bluebird Book
The Wildflower Book — East of the Rockies

BY DONALD AND LILLIAN STOKES/ERNEST WILLIAMS

The Butterfly Book

ALSO BY DONALD STOKES

The Natural History of Wild Shrubs and Vines

The WILDFLOWER BOOK

FROM THE ROCKIES WEST

An Easy Guide to Growing and Identifying Wildflowers

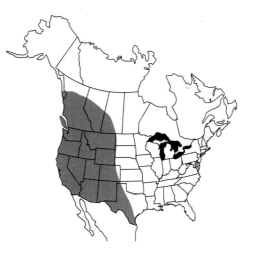

DONALD and LILLIAN STOKES

Little, Brown and Company

Boston   Toronto   London

First edition

Library of Congress Cataloging-in-Publication Data

Stokes, Donald W.
  The wildflower book: from the Rockies West: an easy guide to growing and identifying wildflowers/Donald and Lillian Stokes. — 1st ed.
      p. cm.
    Includes bibliographical references and index.
    ISBN 0-316-81801-1
    1. Wild flower gardening — West (U.S.) 2. Wild flowers — West (U.S.) 3. Wild flowers — West (U.S.) — Identification. 4. Wild flower gardening — Canada, Western. 5. Wild flowers — Canada, Western. 6. Wild flowers — Canada, Western — Identification. I. Stokes, Lillian Q. II. Title.
  SB439.24.W47S76   1993
  635.9′676′0978 — dc20   92-35840

10 9 8 7 6 5 4 3 2 1

RRD-OH

Published simultaneously in Canada by Little, Brown & Company (Canada) Limited

Printed in the United States of America

Photography Acknowledgments

Roger and Donna Aitkenhead: 90 left.
Gwendolyn Brand: 7, 38, 52 left, 65, 69 left, 74 left, 77 right, 81 left, 88.
Kathleen and Lindsey Brown: 6, 46 left, 46 right.
Carlye Calvin: 11, 75 left, 79.
Alan Charnley: 19, 59 left, 67, 69 right.
Raymond Coleman: 8, 77 left.
Kent and Donna Dannen: 76 left, 82 right, 89 right.
Don Eastman: 22 left, 48, 55, 66 right.
Priscilla Eastman: 52 right.
Jessie Harris: 58, 85 right, 85 left.
Peter Lindtner: 57.
Maslowski Photo: 31.
David Middleton: 1, 20, 21, 24, 25, 26, 27 right, 71, 73, 84, 90 right.
Photo/Nats: Philip Beaurline — 92 left; Hal Horwitz — 72 right; Larry Kimball — 78 right; Jeff March — 80 left; A. Peter Margosian — 64 left, 80 right; Jo Ann Ordano — 68 right, 82 left.
C. Gable Ray: 30, 66 left.
John Shaw: 13, 16.
Leroy Simon: 68 left.
Bob Simpson: 59 right.
Bob and Ira Spring: 29, 39 right, 40 right, 47, 75 right, 78 left.
Stokes Nature Company: 32, 33, 34, 35.
Visions From Nature: Dede Gilman — 9, 23, 27 left, 28, 42 bottom, 51, 76 right, 81 right, 83, 86 right; Lee Man Simons — 10.
Visuals Unlimited: Walt Anderson — 17, 54 left, 92 right; Bill Beatty — 44 right; Scott Berner — 14; J. Borsi — 53; Forest Buchanan — 61; Bruce Cushing — 60 right; John Gerlach — 56 right, 62, 63; G. Kirtley-Perkins — 42 top, 70; Link — 39 left; M. Long — 54 right; Steve McCutcheon — 89 left; Glenn Oliver — 40 left, 93; W. Ormerod — 45; Doug Sokell — 37, 60 left, 74 right, 86 left, 87; Ron Spomer — 49; Brooking Tatum — 72 left.
Ernest Williams: 43.
Bob Young: 91.

Contents

THE ROMANCE OF WILDFLOWERS

As Children

For many of us our love of wildflowers began when we were children. We wandered in sunlit meadows and were captivated by the colors, shapes, and scents of the beautiful flowers around us. We watched with curiosity as fuzzy bumblebees gathered pollen, and we ran after butterflies that flew from blossom to blossom as they sipped nectar, the liquid gift of the flowers.

Close-up of an oxeye daisy flowerhead.

We also played games with wildflowers, games that magically predicted our fortunes and future: pulling the petals off a daisy one by one to reveal the true feelings of a loved one while chanting, "She loves me, she loves me not"; studiously holding buttercups under our chins to see if we liked butter as much as we already knew we did; or blowing on dandelion seedheads and counting the seeds that remained to tell us the time of day or how many children we would have.

In addition, we enjoyed the childhood crafts with wildflowers. We wove chains of daisies and clovers into necklaces, bracelets, and garlands to grace our hair. And, occasionally, our small hands gathered bouquets of wildflowers to be presented with pride to those we loved.

As Adults

As adults, most of us still enjoy wildflowers. We search along woodland paths for the earliest treasures of spring, and we are thrilled by the sight of a colorful midsummer meadow. We photograph and paint wildflowers, we arrange cut wildflowers in summer, and we dry wildflowers in fall for winter arrangements. And many of us attempt to grow them on our own property in whatever places they seem to thrive. In short, as adults we try to surround ourselves with wildflowers, indoors and out, in as many ways as we can.

This book has been written to help enrich your experience with wildflowers. We have included chapters on growing wildflowers in meadows, as well as in coastal, mountain, and desert gardens. We show how to incorporate them into existing perennial gardens or use them as landscape elements to conserve water or attract wildlife. We teach you how to grow, preserve, dry, and arrange wildflowers for your home. We explain how to con-

Field of wildflowers including California poppies and goldfields.

serve wildflowers. And we provide a picture gallery of favorite western wildflowers filled with identification clues, cultivation information, and fascinating lore.

We hope this book will help you to fill your life with wildflowers. In so doing, you can bring together the beauty, magic, and romance of wildflowers that you felt as a child with the knowledge and abilities that you have as an adult.

Happy "wildflowering."

Don and Lillian Stokes

WILDFLOWER CONSERVATION

The Ecological View

As the human race matures in its understanding of ecology, it becomes increasingly clear that to save species of plants and animals we must save a critical mass of their environments. Nothing lives in isolation from other things; everything is interconnected.

This is especially true of wildflowers. Many of our native species are dwindling in number as human activity diminishes or destroys their environments. The prairies are a good example; they used to cover millions of acres in the Midwest, but now they can be seen in only a few areas. Accordingly, many of the plants that grew in them are now rare in the wild.

Thus, we must conserve the species *and* the habitats in which they live. To paraphrase the pioneer conservationist Aldo Leopold, "A good tinkerer never loses any of the parts." As we "tinker" with the environment, we should be sure not to lose any of the species that are a part of it.

It is equally true that on a larger scale each habitat is an irreplaceable part of the whole organism we call earth. Acknowledging this view of the earth as an organism is the next step humans need to take and one we are on the threshold of accomplishing.

Some people point out that we need to save wildflowers for the things that they may be able to offer medicine or industry, as if their use to humans is the main reason to save them. An even more important reason is that they are an integral part of our habitat. And when our own habitat is endangered, our survival is in jeopardy.

What Can We Do?

There is no need to feel helpless when it comes to preserving wildflowers, for there are many easy steps that each of us can take, some right in our own backyards.

The first thing to do is join your local wildflower or native plant society. These organizations need your support, and they will also sensitize you to the conservation needs of your area.

Next, look closely at your own backyard. You may be surprised by what is already growing there. We have a swampy area on our property that we rarely venture into, but when we went in to look it over, we found Canada lilies, Jack-in-the-pulpits, and false hellebore already growing there.

The calypso orchid, which can be found in the Northwest.

A meadow of wildflowers in southern California.

In addition to discovering plants, you will most probably want to introduce some additional wildflowers on your property, no matter how small it is. Wildflower gardening is sometimes considered a special sort of hobby, but it is really no different from other gardening; it just happens to focus on native plants. You may want to augment the wildflowers that are already growing at the edge of your lawn; you may want to add wildflowers to a woodsy place where many other plants have trouble growing; or you may want to make a complete wildflower garden or meadow.

Where to Get Wildflowers

If you want to grow wildflowers on your property, you will need to acquire them first. People used to collect plants from the wild, but today this is frowned upon by conservationists. Even when you buy plants from a nursery, you should ask the owner if the plants were nursery-propagated or dug from the wild. You can help preserve wildflowers by being a choosy shopper and by buying only wildflowers from those nurseries and native plant societies that propagate their own wildflowers. (Contact your local native plant society for recommended nurseries — see Resources, page 95.)

In addition, do not pick wildflowers indiscrim-inately, for this can damage the plants and reduce their seed production. And always ask permission before picking flowers from private or public land. Feel free to pick from your own garden, but in the wild, remember that every picked flower means fewer seeds for maintaining that species.

Native Versus Alien

Native wildflowers are species that grow and reproduce in a particular place and were not brought there by humans. *Alien* plants are species that evolved in different habitats or regions and were brought to the new area either inadvertently or on purpose by humans.

The concept of native versus alien is important in wildflower conservation, since habitats are often delicately structured and the introduction of an alien species can upset the structure by crowding out native plants. As you grow wildflowers, continue to increase your awareness of which are native and which are alien. By favoring native species on your property, you can aid in preserving the diverse and complex habitats upon which we all depend.

CREATING WILDFLOWER MEADOWS

The Dream

Flowering meadows are among the most beautiful and romantic wildflower gardens. They evoke images of a carefree existence with clear days, butterflies, picnics, and children picking wildflower bouquets.

These scenes can be yours if you have the right conditions of sun, soil, and moisture and are willing to spend some time in starting and maintaining

California poppies can cover miles of rolling hills.

a meadow garden. All of us would love to have acres of flowering fields, but in reality, a wildflower meadow is a garden and needs continual care. Because of this it is probably best to start with a small area of 50 to 100 square feet and see how it goes.

Choosing a Spot

The first step in creating a wildflower meadow is choosing a location. As with other wildflower habitats, there are four things to check when choosing a spot: the amount of sun it gets, the amount of moisture in the soil, and the texture and acidity of the soil.

The main element needed for a meadow is sun, at least 6–8 hours a day. The more sun, the better the meadow will grow.

Next, dig up a shovelful of soil and feel it. If it is gritty or sandy and light in color, it should be enriched by the addition of humus. Humus is merely decayed vegetation such as compost or peat moss. If the soil is slippery and dense, it may be full of clay. Clay soils do not drain out moisture quickly, and most meadow wildflowers like a well-drained soil. To improve clay soil, add sand and humus. Most meadow wildflowers can survive in a wide range of soils and often do best in average to sandy soils.

Next, check your chosen area for moisture. Is the soil bone dry most of the time? Or is it damp at all times? In either case, certain species can tolerate these conditions better than others. See the lists on page 18 to match species to your type of soil.

Finally, you should check the pH of the soil. As explained on page 22, you can buy a kit at your garden center that will help you do this. Most meadow plants like neutral soils, or those at about 6–8 on the pH scale.

A corner of a meadow with yarrow, black-eyed Susan, and goldenrod.

Three Ways to Create a Wildflower Meadow

How you go about creating your meadow depends on your property, the tools you use, and the amount of time you want to spend. The most color and greatest variety of flowers are created by sowing wildflower seeds; but this is also the most time-consuming approach. Slightly easier, but more expensive, is plugging plants into an existing grassy meadow. And the easiest and least expensive way is through varying your mowing practices on an existing field or meadow.

Method 1: Sowing Seeds

Wildflower meadows can be grown from seed, using a commercial mix or one that you design on your own. But you cannot just sprinkle wildflower seeds on unprepared soil and expect this to result in a gorgeous mass of wildflowers. The earth must be clear of weeds and other competing plants and raked level so that seeds can get good contact with the soil for moisture and nutrients.

Preparing the Soil — There are three ways to prepare soil for seeds: 1) repeated rototilling; 2) rototilling followed by mulching; and 3) rototilling combined with the use of a "safe" herbicide (one that has a short life and low toxicity).

Rotary tilling is used in all three methods because it turns over and uproots existing vegetation, helping to kill it. In a small area, you can turn over the soil by hand. For a slightly larger area, you can buy or rent a small Rototiller. And in even larger areas, you will need to hire someone with a tractor to turn over the soil.

In the first method, thoroughly rototill your area to about 6 inches deep; this may take 2–3 passes of the Rototiller. Then rake the soil, ideally when it is dry, to remove clumps of earth and plant litter and to make the soil surface smooth. After 2–3 weeks, do a shallow rototilling (1 inch deep) to kill

Balsamroot can form wildflower meadows in the Rockies.

other plants that may have grown. Repeat shallow rototillings each 2–3 weeks until you are satisfied that you have killed all or most of the weed seeds in the upper soil layer. Some people water their sites to encourage weed seed growth between rototillings.

The second method also starts with a deep rotary tilling and then raking of the soil. After this, the area should be covered with black plastic and left until fall if you started in spring, or until late spring if you started in fall. The dark plastic absorbs the sun's heat and kills growing plants underneath. After removing the plastic, plant wildflower seeds immediately.

The third method of soil preparation also starts with a thorough rototilling to a depth of 6 inches, followed by raking. After waiting 2–3 weeks for weed seeds or grass rhizomes to grow, spray the area with a glyphosphate herbicide, such as Kleenup or Roundup, to kill actively growing plants. These herbicides are considered safe if used

correctly, for they break down in the soil and become harmless in about 2–3 weeks. If, after 2–3 weeks, weeds and other plants still grow, reapply the herbicide. In any case, be sure to wait at least 2 weeks for the herbicide to break down before planting seeds.

Sowing Seeds — Before sowing seeds, mix them with slightly dampened sand. This keeps the different-size seeds evenly mixed and enables you to see where you have already sown. Mix 5 or more parts sand to each part seeds and dampen with water. Then take the seed-and-sand mixture and scatter it over the ground with a sweeping hand gesture as you walk back and forth over the meadow area.

Next, rake over the soil very lightly to cover most seeds with about ½ inch of soil. After this, tamp down the soil with a roller, with your feet, or with a board that you put down and step on.

Finally, water the seeds and try to keep the ground moist until many of the seeds have germinated, which should be within 1–2 weeks. If you do not have a source of water near your meadow, cover the area with a light mulch of seed-free grasses, such as salt marsh hay, or just hope for periodic showers.

Weeding — When you see little sprouts first start to appear in your meadow area, you may not be able to tell if they are from the seeds you planted or just weeds. But as the plants grow, you may begin to recognize some as weeds, although this takes considerable experience. If you are sure, then start weeding your meadow.

How much you weed a wildflower meadow is up to you and is also affected by the size of your meadow. Since some so-called weeds are native wildflowers, you may want to leave them alone and let them add to your collection. On the other hand, if you have a small meadow and want just the species you planted, then you should look over your plants for weeds about once a week for the first 3 weeks after germination starts, and once every 2 weeks thereafter.

Changes over Time — Your wildflower meadow will change over time. In the first full year after planting, you will see mostly annuals bloom, for

A beautiful mountain meadow scene.

they live only 1 year. In this first year, the biennials (which bloom in their second year and then die) and the perennials (which keep blooming for several years) are growing roots and leaves. In the second year, they will dominate the wildflower meadow. Annuals will show up in the second year only if they find enough bare earth on which to grow from seeds they produced the first year. In the third year, your meadow may be almost all perennials. Grasses and other plants may also move into your meadow over the years.

Some people like the colors of annuals so much that they plant a mix consisting of only annuals each year. Even if you do not use only annuals, you may want to try a new wildflower mix in a year or two. In this case, just prepare the soil as before and sow new seeds over the old meadow area.

Choosing Wildflower Seed Mixes — Many wildflower seed mixes are available in stores and catalogs all across the country. These mixes can be broadly divided into two groups: specialty mixes and regional mixes.

Specialty mixes are for a certain effect or for a certain group of users. They include such categories as flowers that attract hummingbirds, butterflies, or birds; flowers for children; flowers for shade or sun; flowers for moist or dry areas; and just annuals. Regional mixes are collections of seeds designed to be successful for a certain geographic region of the country, such as the Northwest, Rocky Mountains, or Southwest. In some cases, mixes are both regional and specialized, such as northwestern annuals, or southwestern flowers for dry conditions.

Regional seed mixes from reliable companies are a good place to start because they contain wildflowers proven to be successful in your climate and soil conditions. The next step is to read the labels on the packages and see what they tell you about the seeds. The more they tell you, the better you can judge the mix.

Here are some of the things you should look for when reading the label on a wildflower seed mix: the area of ground that the seed mix will cover; the scientific and common names of the flowers; which flowers are annuals, biennials, or perennials; and which plants are native. When comparing seed mixes, choose those with the greatest number of wildflowers native to your region. (For help in recognizing troublesome alien plants, see "Aggressive Alien Plants," page 16.)

In addition, check to see if the mix contains any grass seeds. Grasses are an important part of a natural-looking meadow. However, some grasses spread rapidly and can crowd out wildflowers,

Bluebonnets and Indian paintbrush put on a show in Texas.

A lush mountain meadow scene.

while others form clumps that go nicely between the flowers. Species to avoid in seed mixes include tall fescue, annual rye, orchard grass, and Kentucky bluegrass. Clump-forming grasses that work well in a meadow include little bluestem, side oats grama, switchgrass, June grass, sheep fescue, Indian grass, blue grama, buffalo grass, and Indian ricegrass.

Aggressive Alien Plants

Many of the plants in seed mixtures are not native to North America but were brought here by early settlers and explorers from Central America, Europe, Africa, and Eurasia. Some of these are particularly aggressive and can crowd out native species from certain habitats. When choosing a mix, make certain that these plants do not comprise its majority:

Bachelor's button — *Centaurea cyanus*
Bouncing bet — *Saponaria officinalis*
Butter-and-eggs — *Linaria vulgaris*
Chicory — *Chicorium intybus*
Four-o'clock — *Mirabilis jalapa*
Oxeye daisy — *Chrysanthemum leucanthemum*
Queen Anne's lace — *Daucus carota*
Sweet alyssum — *Lobularia maritima*
Sweet pea — *Lathyrus latifolius*
Tickseed sunflower — *Bidens aristosa*
Yarrow — *Achillea millefolium*

Method 2: Using Grown Plants

If you already have a meadow of grasses, an existing wildflower meadow, or just bare ground, you can add wildflowers by "plugging in" vigorous young plants. You can either buy these plants or grow them from seed and transplant them.

Buying even small wildflower plants is more expensive than sowing seeds, but it is a quick way to get results. When using grown plants, be sure to dig out a hole larger than the size of the pot your flower is in and fill the space with loose earth; this will keep the surrounding vegetation from immediately crowding it out and permits loose soil to make good contact with the plug.

The best way to grow wildflowers from seed for plugging is to use the plastic flats of 6–8 small (about 2 x 2 inches) compartments. Fill the compartments with potting soil and plant 3–4 wildflower seeds in each compartment. When the plants are several inches tall, or have well-developed rosettes (radiating clusters of leaves), you can easily remove them and transplant them safely. Maintain them by watering and keeping competing vegetation back.

Wildflower meadows on top of a mesa.

Method 3: Through Mowing

If your chosen meadow area is covered by tall grass and possibly a few woody shrubs, take a closer look at it. Do you remember seeing any wildflowers here, such as buttercups, daisies, clovers, and other common species? At ground level, do you see any leaves or rosettes of plants other than grasses? Or have you just never looked very closely at this area through a spring and summer?

If the answer is yes to any of these questions, then you may already have a wildflower meadow and not know it. The way to tell for sure is to mow the area at distinct times and see if wildflowers bloom.

First, mow the area to not shorter than 6 inches in fall or early spring and then let it grow without mowing. Keep a list of all the wildflowers that bloom in the area. If, halfway through the summer, it is all grasses, then try mowing again and see if any wildflowers bloom in late summer or fall.

The reason we suggest this is that in most field areas many other plants are growing, but they do not bloom because of competition with the grasses. By mowing in early spring and then in midsummer, you give the competitive edge to the flowers, helping them get enough sun to grow tall and bloom.

In the 2-acre field on our property, we use a variety of mowing practices. We mow some areas

low every 1–2 weeks and keep them as lawn. We let one area grow in spring because it is full of hawkweeds, which bloom then; when they are finished blooming, we mow that area for the rest of the year. Another area grows an abundance of Queen Anne's lace; we stop mowing it in midsummer and have a wonderful show of these flowers. And yet another area has a good natural mix of daisy, winter cress, red clover, buttercup, aster, and thistle; we let this grow all summer and then mow in late fall when all blooming is finished. We leave the unmowed areas in rounded, irregular contours so that they look more natural.

Not enough research has been done to know exactly when to mow a meadow to get the most flowers; thus, we encourage you to experiment with your own field. Certainly, a wildflower meadow of this type is the easiest to maintain and in many ways is the most natural.

Most lawn mowers can mow no higher than 4 inches and so cannot be used for mowing wildflower meadows. Here are some options for the average homeowner. On very small plots, just use grass clippers. On larger plots, use a weed cutter that cuts vegetation with a spinning nylon cord. For areas of an acre or two, a small riding tractor-mower that can be set to 6 inches high is best. For still larger areas, you may need a full-size tractor, or you may have to hire someone who owns one.

Maintaining Your Wildflower Meadow

It is a good idea to mow over your wildflower meadow every year, for this keeps woody plants from getting started. Mowing should be done at least 6 inches high, for this will not disturb the plants that overwinter as leafy rosettes. Again, normal lawn mowers usually cannot be set this high, so you may need to use a weed cutter or small tractor-mower.

In addition, you may want to keep a watchful eye on your meadow over the years to be sure that no undesirable weeds are getting into it.

Some Good Native Wildflowers for Meadows

Coastal Areas

American bistort — *Polygonum bistortoides*
Baby blue-eyes — *Nemophila menziesii*
Black-eyed Susan — *Rudbeckia hirta*
Blanketflower — *Gaillardia aristata*
Blazing star — *Mentzelia lindleyi*
Butterfly weed — *Asclepias tuberosa*
California poppy — *Eschscholtzia californica*
Checkerbloom — *Sidalcea malvaeflora*
Coreopsis — *Coreopsis lanceolata*
Goldenrod — *Solidago* spp.
Goldfields — *Lasthenia californica*
Harebell — *Campanula rotundifolia*
Rocky Mountain iris — *Iris missouriensis*
Scarlet columbine — *Aquilegia formosa*
Washington lupine — *Lupinus polyphyllus*
Western shooting star — *Dodecatheon pulchellum*
Yarrow — *Achillea lanulosa*

Mountain Areas
DRY MEADOWS

Bear grass — *Xerophyllum tenax*
Black-eyed Susan — *Rudbeckia hirta*
Blanketflower — *Gaillardia aristata*
Blue flax — *Linum perenne*
Butterfly weed — *Asclepias tuberosa*
Colorado columbine — *Aquilegia caerulea*
Coreopsis — *Coreopsis lanceolata*
Fireweed — *Epilobium angustifolium*
Goldenrod — *Solidago* spp.
Harebell — *Campanula rotundifolia*
Monkshood — *Aconitum columbianum*
Mule ears — *Wyethia amplexicaulis*
Paintbrush — *Castilleja* spp.
Pasqueflower — *Anemone patens*

Scarlet gilia — *Ipomopsis aggregata*
Sticky geranium — *Geranium viscosissimum*
Scarlet columbine — *Aquilegia formosa*
Yarrow — *Achillea lanulosa*

WET MEADOWS

American bistort — *Polygonum bistortoides*
Cardinal flower — *Lobelia cardinalis*
Elephant's-head — *Pedicularis groenlandica*
Marsh marigold — *Caltha palustris*
Mountain bluebells — *Mertensia ciliata*
Western shooting star — *Dodecatheon pulchellum*
Rocky Mountain iris — *Iris missouriensis*

Dry or Desert Areas

Black-eyed Susan — *Rudbeckia hirta*
Blanketflower — *Gaillardia aristata*
Blazing star — *Mentzelia lindleyi*
Bluebonnet — *Lupinus subcarnosus*
Blue flax — *Linum perenne*
Butterfly weed — *Asclepias tuberosa*
California bluebell — *Phacelia campanularia*
California poppy — *Eschscholtzia californica*
Desert zinnia — *Zinnia grandiflora*
Goldfields — *Lasthenia californica*
Firecracker penstemon — *Penstemon eatonii*
Fireweed — *Epilobium angustifolium*
Harebell — *Campanula rotundifolia*
Tidytips — *Layia platyglossa*
Owl's clover — *Orthocarpus purpurascens*
Pearly everlasting — *Anaphalis margaritacea*
Scarlet gilia — *Ipomopsis aggregata*
Sunflower — *Helianthus annuus*
Yarrow — *Achillea lanulosa*

A hillside of
wildflowers in
Yellowstone.

WOODLAND WILDFLOWER GARDENS

Conditions Needed for a Woodland Wildflower Garden

Woodland wildflowers are among the most beautiful plants in the West. They are adapted to 30 to 40 inches of rain per year, woods with tall trees that create a dappled light underneath, and some topsoil. You will find these conditions in much of the Northwest and northern California and in mountainous areas such as the Rocky Mountains or the Sierra Nevada.

The process of picking a site and preparing the soil for these woodland wildflower gardens is similar no matter where you live; however, the species

Redwood sorrel can be lovely in a woodland garden.

Good Native Wildflowers for Woodland Gardens

For the Northwest and Northern California

Arrowleaf balsamroot — *Balsamorhiza sagittata*
Baby blue-eyes — *Nemophila menziesii*
Blue violet — *Viola adunca*
Dogtooth violet — *Erythronium grandiflorum*
Douglas' iris — *Iris douglasiana*
False Solomon's seal — *Smilacina racemosa*
Heartleaf arnica — *Arnica cordifolia*
Indian pink — *Silene californica*
Leopard lily — *Lilium pardalinum*
Mountain bluebells — *Mertensia ciliata*
Pacific bleeding heart — *Dicentra formosa*
Pasqueflower — *Anemone patens*
Redwood sorrel — *Oxalis oregana*
Scarlet columbine — *Aquilegia formosa*
Sticky geranium — *Geranium viscosissimum*
Wild ginger — *Asarum caudatum*
Yellow skunk cabbage — *Lysichitum americanum*

For the Rocky Mountains

Arrowleaf balsamroot — *Balsamorhiza sagittata*
Blue violet — *Viola adunca*
Colorado columbine — *Aquilegia caerulea*
Dogtooth violet — *Erythronium grandiflorum*
False Solomon's seal — *Smilacina racemosa*
Heartleaf arnica — *Arnica cordifolia*
Monkshood — *Aconitum columbianum*
Mountain bluebells — *Mertensia ciliata*
Pasqueflower — *Anemone patens*
Scarlet columbine — *Aquilegia formosa*
Sticky geranium — *Geranium viscosissimum*

of wildflowers native to each area are slightly different. We have included two lists of wildflowers — one for the Rockies and another for the Northwest and northern California. You will notice that some species can grow in either area.

Picking a Site

There are two ways to pick a site for your woodland wildflowers. One is to go around your property and look for a place with the right conditions; the other is to pick a good potential location in which you want woodland wildflowers to grow and slightly alter it until it meets the right requirements.

An ideal site for woodland wildflowers is in rich soil under tall deciduous trees that let dappled light filter down to the ground. Water should not collect on the site, but neither should the soil be bone dry; and the acidity of the soil should be fairly neutral.

If your chosen site does not have enough light, then you may want to consider removing one or two trees or trimming the lower branches or thinning the crowns of the existing trees. The amount of moisture in the soil and the texture, organic content, and acidity of the soil can be changed later (see "Preparing the Soil," below). The amount of rainwater that gets to the area is harder to regulate without changing the topography of the land.

Planning the Garden

Once you pick the site, you can have the fun of planning your garden. Laying a garden hose on the ground to show the outlines of paths and beds is an easy way to get a sense of how you want to configure your garden beds. Consider creating a path to walk on while you enjoy your wildflowers. You also might want a bench somewhere along the path, facing your favorite view of the garden.

When planning the garden, take into account the heights and blooming times of the plants, with small plants in the front and taller ones toward the back, and with something in bloom during each month of the growing season. Whenever possible, try to create masses of color and foliage by planting groups of each species.

If you do make a path, try to mark the beginning and end of it with a bolder statement, such as a shrub, a special planting, or a large rock on either

Colorado columbine is a favorite for under an aspen grove.

side. Paths can be lined with small rocks or old logs to give them more definition and then covered with pine needles, wood chips, crushed stone, pebbles, or bark mulch.

Preparing the Soil

First of all, try to get a sense of your existing soil by digging out a shovelful from various spots in each proposed flower bed. If you have numerous rocks, then try to remove as many as you can. Small rocks can be used to line an edge of the garden, and large ones can be lifted to the surface and used as a design element in the bed by placing plants in a pleasing relationship to them.

If your soil is divided up or crisscrossed by large roots, then just work with the pockets of soil between them and let spreading plants trail artfully over them.

Next, take a handful of the soil from your future beds and check its texture. Soils have three main textures: *sandy* soil feels gritty and is composed of sand-size particles; *clayey* soil feels smooth or greasy and is made of extremely fine particles; and *loamy* soil contains a mixture of fine and sandlike particles. An easy measure of texture is to take a handful of soil and try to squeeze it into a lump. If it totally falls apart, it is too sandy; if it forms one solid clump, it is too clayey; and if it forms a clump that breaks apart into several clumps when you release it, it is loamy. Almost all plants grow better in loamy soil.

Woodland plants also prefer soil with lots of organic matter, often called *humus*. Humus is decayed animal and plant matter in the form of compost, peat moss, manure, or leaves or shredded bark that has begun to rot. Humus aids essential nutrients and water-absorbing capacity to the soil of a woodland garden.

You can improve sandy soil by adding humus. And you can correct clay soils by adding sand and humus. In either case, be sure to loosen and mix your soil by turning it over with a fork or a small Rototiller before planting.

The last thing to check is the soil's pH — how acid or alkaline it is. The pH scale measures the concentration of hydrogen ions in the soil (*pH* stands for "potential of hydrogen") and ranges from 1 to 14. A pH of 7 is neutral; less than 7 means acid soil, more than 7 means alkaline. Most woodland plants prefer soil that is just about neutral or slightly acid; some need a more acid soil. To test your soil, go to the nearest nursery and buy a small testing kit. Such kits are easy to use and are a good general indicator of pH.

When you know the pH of your soil, you have two choices on how to proceed. You can choose plants that will like your soil just as it is, e.g., acid-loving plants for acidic soil, or you can change the soil to match the plant's requirements. If you want to change your soil and it is too acidic, you can add to it either lime — 5 pounds of ground limestone per 100 square feet will bring the pH of your soil from 5.5 to 6.0 — or compost, which will also help raise the soil's pH. If your soil is too alkaline, you can add sulfur — 2 pounds of sulfur per 100 square feet will bring the pH from 8.0 to 7.0 — or you can add peat moss or rotted pine needles, which will help make the soil more acid.

Planting Wildflowers

Now the real fun begins: deciding which plants you want and where they will go. Woodland wildflowers should be bought from reputable dealers who

Baby blue-eyes can be happy in sunlight or in partial shade.

Heartleaf arnica can brighten up a woodland garden.

Indian pink will bring hummingbirds to your woodland garden.

you are sure do not dig them from the wild, or given to you by friends who divide wildflowers from their own garden. You should never dig plants from the wild except in cases where they will be destroyed by the construction of a road or building, and even then you must have permission of the landowner. For nurseries that carry native plants, see Resources, page 95.

As you select plants, be aware of their growth habits. Some species, such as sticky geranium, spread aggressively. Give these plants room to spread and plant them in places where they will not interfere with other plants. Other species may readily self-sow, and you will need to plan room for their offspring. The Gallery of Favorite Wildflowers, starting on page 36, tells you about the growing habits of many plants.

When buying plants, get three or more of each species so that you can create masses of the same leaves and flowers and create natural-looking groups. Look at the lists in this chapter for some of the easiest plants with which to start.

It is good to have your wildflower garden close to a source of water, for you will need to water the plants during dry spells. Water them individually with a hose in the morning. Using a sprinkler is not as effective; it gets the leaves wet, and its droplets often run off the soil surface. If you have a large garden, you may have to use a sprinkler, and in this case, mulch on the ground keeps the water from running off.

Mulching and Maintenance

Once you have planted and watered your wildflowers, it is a good idea to consider putting a mulch over the bare areas between plants. Mulches serve many important functions: they hold in moisture; they keep weeds from growing; they prevent erosion; they protect the soil from the heat of the midday sun and the cold of the night air; and as they decompose they add humus to the soil.

There are a variety of effective mulches. Several layers (5–10) of newspaper laid over the bare ground and then covered by a thin layer of bark mulch works well and will decompose by the same time next year.

Natural materials for mulching include pine needles (for acid-loving plants), bark mulch, old wood chips (not fresh), chopped-up leaves (one of the best), and dried grass clippings (if they are mixed with other organic material).

If any weeds do grow, they should be pulled up before they have time to go to seed. After a year or two, you may want to divide certain plants that have grown a great deal and replant them in other parts of your garden or give them to a friend just starting out.

DESERT AND DRY-AREA GARDENS

Just Deserts?

Many bona-fide deserts exist in the West, such as the Mojave Desert, Sonoran Desert, Chihuahuan Desert, and areas in the Great Basin. But many areas of the West also have desertlike conditions. If you live in one of these areas, understanding these conditions of climate and soil will help you gauge the needs of native plants and make your wildflower gardens more successful.

This hedgehog cactus brings exciting color to any desert garden.

Dealing With Desertlike Climates

Desertlike climates are characterized by bright sun, strong winds, low humidity, low rainfall, and high daytime temperatures. The vast majority of plants do not favor these conditions, though some are able to flourish in spite of them. There are ways that you can moderate these harsh conditions and make it easier for the native wildflowers you choose to grow.

In desert areas, the sun can be seen from horizon to horizon, creating long, hot days. One of the best ways to protect wildflowers from the sun's heat is to plant trees and shrubs so that you can place the wildflowers in their shade. Ask your local nursery which woody plants are appropriate to your area and choose species that will eventually have a high, filtered shade so that the wildflowers will get dappled sunlight throughout the day.

You can also reduce the baking of the sun by taking advantage of existing structures. For instance, you can place plants on the east or north side of a wall, fence, or your house. This protects the plants from the hottest sunlight during midday and afternoon. Or, you can place plants on north sloping hills, which reduces the angle of the sun on the ground and keeps the ground from getting so hot.

Many desert areas have strong prevailing winds, which in combination with the sun and low humidity, can dry out plants very quickly. Study the wind directions in your property and create windbreaks next to planting areas to protect the wildflowers from drying. These can be plantings of dense shrubs or structures such as wood fences and stone walls. Protection from winds creates a microclimate around the plants that is slightly more humid and reduces evaporation from the plant leaves.

In many desert areas, rainfall is no more than about 10 inches per year, and the rain often comes

Brittlebush can do well in dry, rocky landscapes.

during the winter months. You can help out wildflowers that need more water by placing them in areas where runoff occurs when it rains. This could be at the base of a hill, at the edge of a roof, or where the paving of paths or driveways directs the water.

Preparing Desertlike Soil

Desertlike soil is characterized by its low moisture, low organic content, high heat, high level of salts at the surface, and alkalinity.

Adding organic matter to the soil is one way of increasing the soil's moisture-holding capacity as well as supplying nutrients. However, many desert species of wildflowers are adapted to drier soils and low organic content. Because of this, it is recommended that you add no more than about 30 percent organic matter to your soil, in the form of compost, peat moss, or peat humus. Some gardeners do not add any organic matter; instead, they just put an organic mulch on top of the soil.

Sometimes, growing a desert plant in richer soil makes it lusher at first, but then the plant has trouble retaining moisture during drier times of the year.

Accumulated salts in the upper layer is typical of desert soils. This salt is a product of normal rock erosion where not enough soaking rains wash it down into the lower soil. Plants that absorb too much salt may be stunted or develop yellow leaves. In most cases, the best way to leach these salts into the soil is by giving the garden area a good soaking of water at least once a year.

In some cases, desert soils have a hard layer called caliche, which is often impermeable to water. Before wildflowers are planted in this soil, the caliche needs to be broken up with a pickax. This can be difficult but needs to be done only at the specific place where the flower is planted.

After planting, mulching is a must. Mulch does so many valuable things in gardens that it is amazing we do not all take advantage of it whenever we garden. It protects the earth from heat, it preserves moisture in the soil, it gradually helps enrich the soil, and it prevents weed growth between plants. In the long run, it is a tremendous time saver, reducing the need to weed and water.

Owl's clover can make a dry area look like a beautiful meadow.

Good Plants for Desertlike Gardens

Perennials

Arrowleaf balsamroot — *Balsamorhiza sagittata*
Blanketflower — *Gaillardia aristata*
Blue flax — *Linum perenne*
Blue penstemon — *Penstemon cyaneus*
Brittlebush — *Encelia farinosa*
Butterfly weed — *Asclepias tuberosa*
Desert mallow — *Sphaeralcea ambigua*
Desert marigold — *Baileya multiradiata*
Desert zinnia — *Zinnia grandiflora*
Douglas' wallflower — *Erysimum capitatum*
Firecracker penstemon — *Penstemon eatonii*
Prickly poppy — *Argemone platyceras*
Sulphur flower — *Eriogonum umbellatum*
Wild hyacinth — *Dichelostemma pulchellum*
Yarrow — *Achillea lanulosa*

Annuals

Baby blue-eyes — *Nemophila menziesii*
Blazing star — *Mentzelia lindleyi*
Bluebonnet — *Lupinus texensis*
California bluebell — *Phacelia campanularia*
California poppy — *Eschscholtzia californica*
Desert chia — *Salvia columbariae*
Desert chicory — *Rafinesquia neomexicana*
Desert sand verbena — *Abronia villosa*
Goldfields — *Lasthenia californica*
Sunflower — *Helianthus annuus*
Tidytips — *Layia platyglossa*

Cacti

Buckhorn cholla — *Opuntia acanthocarpa*
Prickly pear cactus — *Opuntia polyacantha*
Strawberry hedgehog cactus — *Echinocereus engelmannii*

In areas where no additional organic matter is needed, a mulch of gravel or crushed stones can be used. Mulches should be 2 to 4 inches thick to be at all effective.

Additional Ways to Conserve Water in Desertlike Wildflower Gardens

Space individual plants far enough apart so that their roots will not compete for the same water. Roots often extend below the ground about as far out (horizontally) as the leaves do above the ground, and this will help you judge a good distance between plants. At the same time, it is smart to group plants in limited areas or islands to maximize their effect and to give you the greatest show for your work.

When grouping plants, take into account the water needs of each species and try to group plants with similar water needs. This will mean that you do not need to give a lot of water to an area where only one plant needs it, while the others could go without watering.

Using a drip hose — one that is closed at one end and has tiny holes all along it where the water drips out — is better for the plants and conserves more water than using a sprinkler. Much of the water from sprinklers evaporates into the air or falls on areas without plants. Water from sprinklers can also pack down the ground surface and then end up running off rather than seeping in.

Tidytips do well in dry or desert gardens.

Desert zinnia is a natural in desert landscapes.

Planting Desert Wildflowers

Perennial desert wildflowers that can be bought from nurseries can be set in the ground after a few days of being left outside to become acclimated to the conditions in your yard. Other desert wildflowers may need to be grown from seed. When growing perennials from seed, start the plants in small flats, where you can control the conditions and give them a healthy start. When they are several inches tall, you can then place them in the ground and give them a good watering.

For annuals, place the seeds in the soil where you want them and avoid transplanting.

Growing Cacti

Cacti are wonderful native plants of deserts and many other habitats. Their structure and form can provide year-round interest in a garden or landscape and their blooms are spectacular. Although cacti can survive warm summers most places, they do not all survive cold winters, so it is best to check with your local nursery to see which ones will be successful in your garden.

Many cacti are collected from the wild. As with all native plants, this practice may put some species in danger of becoming rare. As with all wildflowers, remember to buy only cacti that are nursery grown.

XERISCAPING — CONSERVING WATER

Five Steps

Xeriscaping (pronounced *zer*-i-scap-ing) is a landscaping concept whose main objective is conserving water. Although xeriscaping originated in the West, where water conservation has always been an issue, it is also necessary in the East, where water is rapidly becoming scarce and more expensive. By taking a few sensible steps, you can practically halve the amount of water used to maintain your landscape.

Briefly, here are five ways to conserve water in your landscaping. First, plan your yard carefully, noting where moisture and drought occur naturally and putting appropriate plants in each area. Second, improve soil in all plantings by adding peat moss or humus to help the soil retain moisture. Third, mulch bare ground between and around plants to retain moisture and keep down weeds, which would compete for water. Fourth, limit lawn to where you really need it and replace other areas with good ground covers that need less water. And fifth, select wildflowers that grow naturally in dry areas, for these will be most successful as well as beautiful. For a list of wildflowers that are tolerant of dry conditions, see Desert and Dry-Area Gardens, page 26.

There are many other advantages to designing a water-conserving landscape. One is the reduction of maintenance chores such as weeding and watering. Mulches, if 2 to 3 inches deep, can inhibit all weeds from growing between plants, and this can save hours of midsummer weeding. Mulches also hold almost all the moisture in the soil, greatly reducing the amount of time and money spent watering your garden.

In addition, mulches and proper plant choice will result in healthier plants. The mulch layer keeps the soil loose by encouraging earthworm activity near the surface. It protects the roots from the baking hot sun. And, it gradually adds rotted organic matter to the soil.

Therefore, whether you live in an area with a little water or a lot of water, it pays to practice the principles of xeriscaping.

Sulphur flower does not need much water to thrive.

WILDFLOWERS IN THE ROCK GARDEN

Rock Gardens Are a Natural for the West

Rock gardens are a wonderful way to enjoy the wildflowers that grow naturally in the alpine zones of the many mountainous areas of the West. Rock gardens are usually fairly small gardens on a slight slope with a collection of large and small rocks placed in an artistic arrangement. The soil should be well-drained, which can be achieved by mixing equal parts of loam, peat moss, and sand.

Alpine plants are a natural for these gardens since their own environment is one of rocks, sun, and a sandy soil with very little organic matter. They are usually low-growing, with small leaves that form a rounded, cushion-shape plant. This shape conserves heat and moisture.

The plants listed at right are native to the West and will be very happy in your rock garden. Since these plants are small, a special setting where they are grouped together and can be seen on a slope highlights their beauty.

Native Wildflowers for Rock Gardens

Alpine sunflower — *Hymenoxys grandiflora*
Bitterroot — *Lewisia rediviva*
Desert marigold — *Baileya multiradiata*
Desert zinnia — *Zinnia grandiflora*
Fairy primrose — *Primula angustifolia*
Lance-leaf stonecrop — *Sedum lanceolatum*
Moss campion — *Silene acaulis*
Queen's crown — *Sedum rhodanthum*
Sky pilot — *Polemonium viscosum*
Sulphur flower — *Eriogonum umbellatum*
White phlox — *Phlox multiflora*
Wild hyacinth — *Dichelostemma pulchellum*

Moss campion is an alpine plant that does well in rock-garden settings.

WILDFLOWERS FOR WILDLIFE

More Than Beauty

Beauty is not the only reward of planting wildflowers; there are also all of the birds and butterflies that the flowers attract. In fact, certain wildflowers are particularly alluring to butterflies, songbirds, or hummingbirds, and if you plant these, you have a good chance of tempting these delightful visitors into your yard.

Butterflies and hummingbirds come to flowers to drink the nectar in the blossoms. Although hummingbirds will feed at just about any flower that offers nectar, they are especially attracted to long, red, tubular flowers. The long tubes and horizontal or downward orientation of these flowers favor the hovering hummingbird with its long tongue and makes it hard for insects to land on the flower and reach the nectar.

Butterflies feed on a wide variety of wildflowers, but there are certain ones that they seem to love most. No one characteristic clearly distinguishes these flowers; they are just the ones at which observers have most often seen butterflies.

In addition to hummingbirds, your garden can attract other small birds, which come to eat the seeds or berries produced by the wildflowers. Finches, such as goldfinches, purple finches, and pine siskins, like seeds and often land on the flowerheads to feed. Other birds, such as juncos and a variety of sparrows, will feed on the seeds that have fallen from the flowers onto the ground. In our garden, we leave flower stalks standing throughout winter, and we always find these species visiting those spots. Wildflowers that produce berries, such as baneberry and bunchberry, may attract fruit-eating birds, such as mockingbirds, cardinals, cedar waxwings, robins, and many others. Chipmunks will also feed on these berries.

When you see wildflowers attracting other wildlife, it is a reminder of the interconnectedness of nature. Wildflowers depend on their pollinators to enable them to produce seeds, and in turn, the pollinators depend on the flowers' nectar as food. In addition, the berry-producing wildflowers count on birds to disperse their seeds as they eat the berries and void the seeds in new places.

The lists on the opposite page include wildflowers that attract birds and butterflies.

This American copper was attracted by the nectar in butterfly weed.

Goldfinches will come to eat the seeds on purple coneflower.

Wildflowers That Attract Hummingbirds

Cardinal flower — *Lobelia cardinalis*
Desert paintbrush — *Castilleja chromosa*
Firecracker penstemon — *Penstemon eatonii*
Fireweed — *Epilobium angustifolium*
Indian pink — *Silene californica*
Monkey flower — *Mimulus cardinalis*
Pacific bleeding heart — *Dicentra formosa*
Scarlet gilia — *Ipomopsis aggregata*
Western columbine — *Aquilegia formosa*

Wildflowers That Attract Seed- or Berry-Eating Birds

Black-eyed Susan — *Rudbeckia* spp.
Coreopsis — *Coreopsis* spp.
False Solomon's seal — *Smilacina racemosa*
Lupines — *Lupinus* spp.
Purple coneflower — *Echinacea purpurea*
Redwood sorrel — *Oxalis oregana*
Sulphur flower — *Eriogonum umbellatum*
Sunflower — *Helianthus* spp.
Thistle — *Cirsium* spp.

Wildflowers That Attract Butterflies

Black-eyed Susan — *Rudbeckia* spp.
Blanketflower — *Gaillardia* spp.
Butterfly weed — *Asclepias tuberosa*
Coreopsis — *Coreopsis* spp.
Cosmos — *Cosmos bipinnatus*
Forget-me-not — *Myosotis sylvatica*
Gayfeather — *Liatris* spp.
Goldenrod — *Solidago* spp.
Joe-Pye weed — *Eupatorium* spp.
Lily — *Lilium* spp.
Milkweed — *Asclepias* spp.
Oxeye daisy — *Chrysanthemum leucanthemum*
Phlox — *Phlox* spp.
Purple coneflower — *Echinacea purpurea*
Queen Anne's lace — *Daucus carota*
Sneezeweed — *Helenium autumnale*
Sunflower — *Helianthus* spp.
Thistle — *Cirsium* spp.
Yarrow — *Achillea lanulosa*

ARRANGING WILDFLOWERS

Double Pleasure

One of the most beautiful ways to enjoy and appreciate wildflowers is to go into your field or garden and gather bunches to fill vases and use in arrangements. Thus, not only do your wildflowers provide you with the beauty of nature outdoors, but you also get the pleasure of having the lovely arrangements decorate the inside of your home.

Cut wildflowers can be enjoyed in both their fresh and dried states. We love to fill our home with fresh flowers during the summer growing season. In winter we dress up the house with a variety of beautiful dried arrangements and even incorporate dried flowers into the Christmas wreath we hang on our door.

Collecting Wildflowers

Although picking wildflowers may seem like a simple matter, there are some guidelines you should follow to protect the plants and make the task easier for yourself.

Pick wildflowers only from your own property or from other areas where you have the permission of the landowner. Do not pick wildflowers on public or protected lands (in some states it is illegal to pick wildflowers from along public roads). Do not pick endangered species (your State Natural Heritage Program will supply you with a list of endangered species in your region). Identify the species you are picking by using this guide or another wildflower guide. (See Resources, page 94.)

When gathering wildflowers, do not remove all the blooms from a plant; leave some blooms so the plant can set seed and reproduce. Never pull the plant up by its roots.

Cut the stem with a sharp knife or clippers and remove any excess leaves or dead stalks. This is often done more easily on the spot than in your home. Place newly cut fresh flowers in a container partially filled with water. We find that a bucket or a plastic 1-gallon milk container with the top cut off makes a good carrying container.

A lovely wildflower arrangement.

Some cut flowers waiting to be used in arrangements.

Arranging Fresh Flowers

When you arrive home, the creative fun begins as you decide how to use all the beautiful flowers. You may choose to make an informal bouquet by merely putting the flowers in a vase with water, or you might decide to design a more formal arrangement. We keep a large collection of vases and containers of different colors and materials for just this purpose. It is fun to coordinate the colors of the flowers with those of the vase and then place the arrangement in just the right setting.

To make an arrangement, you will need a block of "oasis," a foam brick that absorbs water and holds the flower stems in place. Soak the oasis in water for about ½ hour before using. Cut the oasis so that it fits inside the container and protrudes about 2 inches above it. Replenish the water in the oasis daily to keep the flowers fresh.

Cut flower stems at an angle — to absorb more water — and to the correct length for the arrangement you are creating. A general rule of thumb is to make the arrangement 1½ times higher than the container. Experiment with different forms and colors of flowers to see what pleases you. Flower arranging is an art that is mastered over time, and every time you make an arrangement you will learn something new.

Arranging Dried Flowers

Dried arrangements add beauty to your home in fall and winter and will last for many months. Making an arrangement with dried flowers is similar to making a fresh flower arrangement. However, dried arrangements do not require water, and this leaves you with a greater choice of containers. Be inventive. Baskets, seashells, pieces of driftwood, and many other objects can make wonderful containers for your dried flowers.

An oasis block is useful for dried arrangements also, for it holds the flower stems in place. Obviously, you should not soak the oasis before using it. Oasis foam bricks are available in brown as well as green, and the brown may blend better with dried arrangements. Handle the dried material carefully, since it is brittle and more fragile than fresh material. Consider using dried grasses and seedpods to add variety to your arrangements.

The next chapter explains how to dry flowers.

DRYING WILDFLOWERS

Lasting Treasures

Using dried wildflowers is an excellent way to bring beauty and color into your home all year round. A beautiful dried arrangement can dress up a table, serve as a centerpiece, or brighten a corner. Dried flowers can be used in wreaths and bouquets, and dried petals in potpourris. You can also press flowers and use them to make greeting cards, framed pictures, bookmarks, and other craft projects. You are limited only by your imagination.

Drying Flowers

Drying flowers is both easy and fun. First, collect flowers following the methods described in the previous chapter. Then strip most of the lower leaves

Pretty arrangements can also be made with dried wildflowers.

off and remove any water or moisture from the stems, foliage, and flowers. From this point, you have several methods of drying flowers from which to choose: hanging, drying flat, or using a desiccant.

Hanging

Tie flowers of the same species in bunches by securing the bottoms of their stems with rubber bands. Hang the flowers upside down out of direct sunlight and in a dry place with good ventilation and air circulation. Do not make the bunches too large or hang them so closely together that air cannot adequately circulate. Bunches may be hung from coat hangers, drying racks, or from nails hammered into rafters. It takes flowers from several days to a week to dry by this method.

Drying Flat

You can also dry flowers by laying them flat on slatted shelves, trays with screen bottoms, or newspaper-covered trays. (Do not crowd the flowers on the trays.) Place trays in a warm, dry place. When thoroughly dried, the flowers should feel crisp. It takes flowers approximately 1 week to dry. This method works best for drying loose petals.

Additionally, flowers can be dried in about 1 hour when placed on a cookie sheet in an oven set to the lowest heat with the door propped open. This method should be used with extreme care and only by responsible adults.

Using a Desiccant

Finally, cut flowers may be dried by placing them in a desiccant, which is an absorbent powdery material such as silica gel or a mixture of 3 parts borax to 10 parts white cornmeal. Flowers dried in this manner retain their color and structure better than with other drying methods.

A drying rack, flower press, and desiccant for drying wildflowers.

Silica gel, available from garden shops and florists, is the most expensive desiccant but is very effective and easily used. It can be reused indefinitely if dried out in an oven at low temperature after use. It turns white when it absorbs moisture but reverts to its blue color when dry.

When using a desiccant, remove stems from flowers to be dried. (They can be given false stems when dry by inserting florist's wire into the base of the bloom.) Put a 1-inch layer of desiccant into an airtight container and lay the flowers on top. In general, lay blossoms faceup. Certain large blooms, such as lilies, can be filled with desiccant first and placed faceup. Some flowers that are flat-petaled, such as daisies, are best dried facedown.

Cover the flowers completely by gently pouring desiccant over them. Cover the container tightly and place it in a warm, dry place. Drying times vary from 2 days to 2 weeks, depending on the flower species. Flowers are done when they feel dry and papery.

Pressing Wildflowers

Pressed wildflowers make beautiful decorations. To press, gather wildflowers on a dry, sunny day when they are at their peak bloom. Select freshly opened, perfect blossoms. Flowers with heads that can be easily flattened work best. Some flowers press better when separated from their stems.

Press flowers between layers of good absorbent paper with firm and constant pressure for about 6 weeks. Old phone books are ideal because their paper is of the right absorbency and they contain many pages. Place as many flowers as will fit on a page, and put several pages between each layer of flowers. Put weight, such as bricks, on the phone book to help press the flowers.

You also may purchase a flower press or construct your own. Use 2 pieces of plywood 9 inches square and ½ inch thick. Drill holes at each corner of the press and put 3-inch bolts through the holes and secure them with wing nuts. Press flowers in between 2 sheets of blotting paper (such as that used on desktops) and separate each layer of flowers from the next with a sheet of cardboard. Tighten the wing nuts to apply pressure to the sandwiched layers of flowers. Flowers take about 10 days to 6 weeks to dry.

Arrange pressed flowers in artistic combinations by gluing them on cards, bookmarks, or any kind of fabric or paper. Use a toothpick to apply a latex adhesive to the flowers. Protect your designs with clear varnish, acetate, coating resin, glass, or clear self-sticking adhesive covering film. Your creations will make beautiful, long-lasting treasures or gifts.

GALLERY OF FAVORITE WILDFLOWERS

Lore, Identification, and Growing Tips

The following section illustrates 85 favorite western wildflowers. We realize that this is only a fraction of the species in this region. Because of the limitations of space, many hard choices had to be made. Our hope is that we have covered most of your favorites.

The flowers are arranged by color, and within each color section, flowers with similarities are grouped together whenever possible. We follow this sequence: white, yellow, orange, red, blue, and pink.

To identify a flower in the field, look through the appropriate color section; to look up a flower for other information, use the index at the back of the book.

Accompanying each picture is text that describes lore, identification, habitat, range in western North America, origin, height, blooming period, and information on growing.

Some of the terms used in the sections giving identification clues may be unfamiliar to you; the glossary on page 94 defines many of these commonly used terms.

Each section of growing tips starts with the plant's light and soil requirements. We have made an effort to simplify the terms normally used to describe these conditions.

The three categories of light we have used are *shade* (very little direct sun); *part shade* (dappled light or sun for fewer than 5 hours a day); and *full sun* (direct sun for 6 or more hours daily).

Soil can be classified according to four important qualities: texture, pH, organic content, and moisture. Most plants prefer a soil that has a loamy texture and is neutral in pH (pH 6.5–7.5). For a discussion of this, see "Preparing the Soil," page 21. Plants that have special pH requirements are so noted in the Gallery.

Organic content is the amount of rotted plant or animal material in the soil and can be roughly determined by the soil's color. Soil *low* in organic matter is poor soil, and its color is tan; *average* soil is moderate in organic matter, and its color is brown; *rich* soil is filled with organic matter and is dark brown in color.

The moisture content of soil is determined by topography, with water flowing away from high areas and collecting in low areas, and by soil texture, with sandy soils draining rapidly and clayey soils holding moisture. We have divided soil moisture requirements into three types: *low* — soil is dry most of the time; *average* — soil is moist about half the time; and *high* — soil is usually moist.

SACRED DATURA is unusual in that its large, white flowers open at dusk and close as the sun hits them the following morning. This habit is due to its being pollinated by hawk or hummingbird moths. These are large moths that hover in front of flowers at night, sucking nectar through their long mouthparts, which they uncoil and place way into the heart of the flower.

Identification clues: A sprawling plant with blue-green leaves; its distinctive flowers are white, 4–8 inches wide and 6–10 inches long. Flowers turn purple to brown after being open for the night.

Where found: Dry, open areas; throughout the Southwest. Native.

Height: 6–12 inches.   **In bloom:** May–October.

Growing tips: *Light needs* — full sun; *soil needs* — low to average organic content, low to average moisture. Due to the poisonous nature of the plant parts, you may not wish to add it to your garden. Perennial.

Sacred datura — *Datura meteloides*

Ajo lily —
Hesperocallis
undulata

AJO LILY is named for the Spanish word for garlic, since this is what it looked like to early Spanish explorers who saw the Native Americans eating it. The bulb is hard to collect since it can be 1–2 feet beneath the surface. In years when winters are dry, very few ajo lilies bloom, but after wet winters, the flowering stalks are abundant in the desert, and each stalk has several blooms, giving off a pleasant fragrance.

Identification clues: Long, wavy-margined, narrow leaves at base of plant; flowers are large, white, and trumpet-shape and are at the top of a 6–24 inch stem.

Where found: Deserts; southern California and Arizona. Native.

Height: 6–24 inches.   **In bloom:** February–May.

Growing tips: *Light needs* — full sun; *soil needs* — poor to average organic content, low to average moisture. Bulb grows deep in the soil. Perennial.

WESTERN TRILLIUM is one of only two species of trilliums native to the West. In the East, where trilliums probably originated, many more species exist. Trilliums take 6 to 8 years to grow from seed to first flowering — one reason why it is so important to preserve them in the wild.

Identification clues: Three large, ovate leaves atop a stem; flower is white with 3 large petals and is positioned in the center of the 3 leaves.

Where found: Rich woods and boggy areas; from British Columbia to Montana south to northern California and Colorado. Native.

Height: 8–16 inches.   **In bloom:** March–June.

Growing tips: *Light needs* — part shade; *soil needs* — rich organic matter, average to high moisture. This is not a plant that should be bought from nurseries, for it is almost always dug from the wild. If you are lucky enough to have some growing on your property, be sure that it is not too crowded by other plants. Perennial.

Western trillium — *Trillium ovatum*

Bitterroot — *Lewisia rediviva*

BITTERROOT is the state flower of Montana. Its genus name honors Captain Meriwether Lewis of Lewis and Clark fame, who collected bitterroot in 1806 on one of his explorations. Native Americans have long collected the root in early spring, when only the leaves appear, and then peeled, boiled, and ground the root into meal. The bitterness of the roots is removed by cooking.

Identification clues: Distinctive, large, white to pink flower 1–2 inches across. The plant looks leafless since its leaves appear for only a short time before the flower opens and then they die back. Several other species of *Lewisia* exist, but none has the large flower and the seeming lack of leaves.

Where found: Rocky flats and slopes; from western Montana to southern British Columbia south to northern Colorado and southern California. Native.

Height: 1–4 inches.   **In bloom:** March–July.

Growing tips: *Light needs* — full sun; *soil needs* — low to average organic content, low moisture. Needs moisture only in spring when first flowering; after that it should remain fairly dry. Can withstand cold temperatures. Good for rock gardens. Perennial.

Marsh marigold — *Caltha leptosepala*

MARSH MARIGOLD is one of the first plants to bloom in moist, mountain meadows after the snow recedes; in some cases, it may even push up through the last inch or two of snow. Despite the poisonous alkaloids in its leaves, elk regularly feed on this plant without harm. Two of its other common names are cowslip and elk's lip.

Identification clues: Large, shiny, rounded basal leaves; large white flowers with a conspicuous yellow center — generally 1 per stalk. Flowers can have 5 or more petal-like sepals. A similar species in coastal ranges and Colorado and Utah is *C. biflora*; it often has 2 flowers per stalk.

Where found: Wet, mountain meadows; from Alaska and western Canada south into New Mexico. Native.

Height: 6–12 inches.   **In bloom:** May–August.

Growing tips: *Light needs* — part shade to full sun; *soil needs* — average to rich organic content, high moisture. This plant needs water in the soil at all times. It is vigorous in spring, but may die back by late summer with just its roots and crown overwintering. Can be divided (cutting the root mass vertically into two or more divisions that can be separately planted) after blooming. Perennial.

SEGO LILY is one of the mariposa lilies and has intricate designs at the base of its 3 beautiful petals. This species is the state flower of Utah, and the hardened corm at its base was collected and used as food by Native Americans, as well as by early Mormons who traveled to the West. Sego is a Native American name for the plant.

Identification clues: Thin, grasslike leaves; flowers have 3 large, white petals and are at the tips of stalks. Each petal at its base has a yellow spot with a dark red bar above it.

Where found: Plains, hillsides, open areas at low elevations; from Idaho and California south to northern New Mexico. Native.

Height: 6–18 inches.   **In bloom:** May–July.

Growing tips: *Light needs* — full sun; *soil needs* — low to average organic content, low to average moisture. Generally not used as a garden plant; instead, enjoy them in the wild. Perennial.

Sego lily — *Calochortus nuttallii*

Prickly poppy — *Argemone platyceras*

PRICKLY POPPIES are common western plants of rangelands, roadsides, and other disturbed areas. They are tall and can be found opening their large-petaled blooms in any month of the year in the Southwest and in spring and summer in northern areas. Although not considered a treasured wildflower, they are hardy and beautify many areas that would otherwise look barren.

Identification clues: Numerous spines on the leaves, stems, and buds; 5 large, white, tissue paper–like petals around a center of dense, pollen-laden stamens. Although many species can be found, this is one of the loveliest.

Where found: Plains, rangeland, roadsides, and other disturbed areas; from South Dakota and Wyoming to Texas and southern California. Native.

Height: 1–4 feet. **In bloom:** All year.

Growing tips: *Light needs* — full sun; *soil needs* — low to average organic content, low to average moisture. This hardy plant is a good candidate for adding some beauty and background height to a water-conserving garden. Perennial.

Oxeye daisy — *Chrysanthemum leucanthemum*

OXEYE DAISIES originated in Asia and, from there, spread to mainland Europe and then to England. They were probably transported to North America as seeds brought in the grain or hay carried on early colonists' boats. Oxeye daisies contributed to the hybrid garden flower known as shasta daisy.

Identification clues: Leaves at base and on stem are narrow and have shallow lobes; each flowerhead has white ray flowers surrounding a center of yellow disk flowers.

Where found: Meadows, roadsides, waste spaces; throughout the West. Originally from Asia.

Height: 1–2 feet.   **In bloom:** June–August.

Growing tips: *Light needs* — full sun; *soil needs* — from low to rich organic content, average moisture. Readily self-seeds, and seedlings can be easily transplanted. Divide in spring or fall. Perennial.

Desert chicory — *Rafinesquia neomexicana*

DESERT CHICORY, in its native habitat of deserts, blooms early in spring, but only if the winter has been wet. In some years with dry winters, it may not flower. Its seeds are like those of dandelions, each with a tuft of dispersal hairs that carries it along on the winds. It is named in honor of Constantine Rafinesque, an American botanist who lived in the early 1800s.

Identification clues: Narrow, dandelion-like leaves; flowers white with square-tipped petals.

Where found: Desert areas; western Texas to southern California. Native.

Height: 6–20 inches.   **In bloom:** March–May.

Growing tips: *Light needs* — full sun to part shade; *soil needs* — low to average organic content, low to average moisture. Annual.

White phlox — *Phlox multiflora*

WHITE PHLOX is a lovely plant of the mountains and can be particularly beautiful when it grows in alpine regions with moss campion, another cushionlike plant. The pink flowers and white flowers form a lovely contrast. Phlox flowers have a fairly long tube beneath their 5 petals which limits access to their nectar to moths and butterflies that have long mouthparts.

Identification clues: Leaves are short and linear; flowers are white with 5 petals; the whole plant forms a rounded, cushionlike shape.

Where found: Dry ridges, open woods, alpine areas; from Idaho to Montana south to Nevada and New Mexico. Native.

Height: 2–4 inches.   **In bloom:** May–July.

Growing tips: *Light needs* — part shade to full sun; *soil needs* — average organic content, average moisture. Many phloxes are available through nurseries and work well in rock gardens since they are small and low to the ground. Perennial.

American bistort — *Polygonum bistortoides*

AMERICAN BISTORT can be very abundant and cover large areas of wet meadows. One aspect of the plant you cannot see is its thick, twisted root, for which it has been nicknamed snakeroot. The root was used as a food by Native Americans, either roasted or boiled.

Identification clues: Basal leaves lancelike and with long petioles; smaller leaves clasp stem; flowers are white to pink and clustered into a dense mass at the tips of stalks.

Where found: Wet meadows from coastal marshes to above timberline; from Montana to British Columbia south to California and Mexico. Native.

Height: 6–24 inches.   **In bloom:** June–August.

Growing tips: *Light needs* — full sun; *soil needs* — average to rich organic content, average to high moisture. Perennial.

PEARLY EVERLASTING gets its name from the color of its flowers and its long-lasting blooms. If you grow it in your garden, you can then pick the flower stalks and hang them upside down to dry. They keep their color and look lovely in dried arrangements.

Identification clues: Vertical stalks with narrow, grasslike leaves that are hairy on the underside; small, pearly flowers are clustered together at the top of the stalk.

Where found: Open areas, roadsides, hillsides, burned areas, and other disturbed sites; from southern Alaska through Canada and California and into northern New Mexico. Native.

Height: ½–3 feet.   **In bloom:** June–September.

Growing tips: *Light needs* — part shade to full sun; *soil needs* — low to rich organic content, low to high moisture. From its growing requirements, it is obvious that pearly everlasting is adaptable. It looks excellent in rock gardens and spreads through underground rhizomes. Can be divided in spring. Perennial.

Pearly everlasting — *Anaphalis margaritacea*

False Solomon's seal —
Smilacina racemosa

FALSE SOLOMON'S SEAL has something to offer the wildflower lover throughout the growing season: in spring, it has graceful arching stems with attractive leaves; in summer, it has showy flowers; and in fall, it has a large cluster of bright red berries. A similar, smaller species is starry false Solomon's seal, S. *stellata*, whose berries, instead of being red, are dark red to maroon with black stripes.

Identification clues: Alternate, parallel-veined leaves on a slightly zigzag, arching stem; white flowers at the tip of the stem.

Where found: Woods; from Southern Alberta and British Columbia south to central California and western Texas. Native.

Height: 1–3 feet. **In bloom:** May–July.

Growing tips: *Light needs* — part shade; *soil needs* — rich organic content, average to high moisture. This plant prefers slightly acidic soil but will grow under a variety of conditions. Good foliage plant in shaded locations. Spreads by growth of rhizomes. Perennial.

Queen Anne's lace — *Daucus carota*

QUEEN ANNE'S LACE, also called wild carrot, is the species from which present-day carrots were developed. When crushed, the leaves smell like carrot leaves, and there is a tough carrotlike taproot. Attractive dried winter seedheads open and close with changes in humidity. Dip a dry one in water and watch it close up.

Identification clues: Basal rosette of fernlike leaves in first 1–2 years; 2nd–3rd year grows a branching stalk with white, flat-topped clusters of flowers at the tips.

Where found: Fields, roadsides, waste spaces; throughout the West. Originally from Europe.

Height: 2–4 feet.   **In bloom:** April–September; all year in Pacific states.

Growing tips: *Light needs* — full sun; *soil needs* — low to rich organic content, average moisture. Needs two years to flower and then dies, but can self-seed. Good for meadows and perennial gardens. Biennial.

YARROW leaves, in the past, were steeped in water to make a tea that supposedly could help cure, among other things, baldness and the common cold, although both maladies obviously persist. The dried seedheads are sometimes used as miniature trees on architects' models of buildings.

Identification clues: Finely cut, fernlike leaves at the base and along the flower stalk; dense, flattopped cluster of flowers at tip of stem. Crushed leaves smell medicinal. A nearly identical introduced species is also called yarrow (*A. millefolium*) and is more commonly found in the East.

Where found: Fields, roadsides, waste spaces; throughout the West. Native.

Height: 1–4 feet.   **In bloom:** June–September.

Growing tips: *Light needs* — full sun; *soil needs* — low to rich organic content, low to average moisture. Good for meadows, although can spread aggressively. A water-conserving species well-adapted to poor soils. Divide in spring or fall. Perennial.

Yarrow — *Achillea lanulosa*

Bear grass — *Xerophyllum tenax*

BEAR GRASS is one of the more striking flowers found in northern mountainous areas of the West. It is a member of the lily family, but when not in flower, its leaves can easily be mistaken for grasses. It does not bloom every year, and blooms even less frequently in more shaded sites. The leaves are slippery and pull out from the plant when stepped on; they have been used by Native Americans for weaving baskets.

Identification clues: Bunches of grasslike basal leaves; flowers are white and clustered at the top of a tall stalk, making it look like a white club.

Where found: Open forests or alpine slopes; from Alberta to British Columbia south to California and Wyoming. Native.

Height: 1–5 feet.   **In bloom:** May–August.

Growing tips: *Light needs* — part shade to full sun; *soil needs* — average organic content, low to average moisture. Can withstand dry conditions. Spreads by tough rhizomes, which send up new clusters of leaves nearby. Perennial.

Mule ears — *Wyethia amplexicaulis*

MULE EARS is an expressive name that describes the shape of this plant's leaves. This wildflower is common in the northern Rockies and often competes with grasses in rangelands and has, therefore, been subject to various eradication programs. The genus name is in honor of Captain Nathaniel Wyeth, who led botanical expeditions and established a fort and fur trading post in the Northwest.

Identification clues: Basal leaves 12–15 inches long, lancelike, and glossy; flowers are yellow, sunflowerlike, 2–3 inches across. Arrowleaf balsamroot (*Balsamorhiza sagittata*) is similar but has arrowhead-shape leaves. There are two other species in the same range: *W. scabra* and *W. helianthoides*, or white wyethia. The first has rough, hairy leaves, and the second has white flowers.

Where found: Open, grassy spots in mountainous areas; from Washington to Montana south to Nevada and Colorado. Native.

Height: 1–2 feet.   **In bloom:** May–July.

Growing tips: *Light needs* — full sun; *soil needs* — average to rich organic content, low to high moisture. Spreads by seed. Perennial.

Heartleaf arnica —
Arnica cordifolia

HEARTLEAF ARNICA is one of the many yellow-flowered plants in the West that resemble sunflowers. Its seeds look like those of dandelions in that they have a little parasol of filaments that disperse them on the wind. The crushed, dried leaves of arnica have been used for centuries as a disinfectant, and fresh leaves rubbed over sore spots may be soothing.

Identification clues: Paired, heart-shape leaves at the base of the plant; a single, daisylike flower at the top of the stem. Flower is all yellow and 2–3 inches across. This is the most common arnica, but several other species exist, all with paired leaves at the base of the stem.

Where found: Moist, open woods of aspens or pines; from Alaska to Michigan and south to southern California and northern New Mexico. Native.

Height: 8–24 inches.   **In bloom:** May–August.

Growing tips: *Light needs* — part shade; *soil needs* — average to rich organic content, average to high moisture. A lovely plant for adding color to partly shaded areas under pines or aspens. Readily self-seeds. Perennial.

**Alpine sunflower —
*Hymenoxys grandiflora***

ALPINE SUNFLOWER is easy to recognize because it is the largest bloom in alpine areas. In fact, the size of the flower looks disproportionately large, since the whole plant remains under a foot tall. But the plant has no need to be taller, since all the competition is also short. Its height and the hairs on its thin leaves and stems probably help it preserve moisture in the harsh alpine climate. A charming habit of this wildflower is that the large blooms tend to face east.

Identification clues: A short plant with thin, much divided leaves; leaves and stems are covered with short hairs; flowers are 3–4 inches across, daisylike, and all yellow.

Where found: Dry, rocky slopes or alpine flats above 4,000 feet; in Rocky Mountains from southern Montana south to New Mexico; also in dry California mountains. Native.

Height: 6–12 inches. **In bloom:** June–September.

Growing tips: *Light needs* — full sun; *soil needs* — low to average organic content, low to average moisture. This plant lives in gravelly soil of neutral pH, so try to create these conditions where you plant it. It does well in a rock garden. It can be grown from seed, but takes a year to reach blooming age. Perennial.

Arrowleaf balsamroot — *Balsamorhiza sagittata*

ARROWLEAF BALSAMROOT is common throughout much of the West and is one of the many wildflowers that look like "sunflowers." Balsamroots have only basal leaves, and their flowers are on separate stalks, unlike true sunflowers, which have leaves only on their flower stalk. The common and scientific names of balsamroot come from the arrowlike shape of the leaves and the balsamlike odor of the roots. Grazing wildlife and livestock often feed on the plant, and Native Americans used the young shoots, root, and seeds as food.

Identification clues: Long, arrow-shape, silvery leaves at the base; flower stalk generally is without leaves and is topped by sunflower-like flowers 2–4 inches across. Some other balsamroot species are similar, except their leaves are toothed rather than smooth, as is the case with this species.

Where found: From sagebrush plains to pine forests and rocky areas at higher elevations; from British Columbia to South Dakota south to California and Colorado. Native.

Height: ½–2 feet.   **In bloom:** April–July.

Growing tips: *Light needs* — part shade to full sun; *soil needs* — average organic content, low to average moisture. Perennial.

Tidytips — *Layia platyglossa*

TIDYTIPS is perfectly named, for the tips of its petal-like ray flowers look as if they have been neatly dipped in white paint. The genus is named after George Tradescant Lay, a botanist who roamed over California in the 1800s. Tidytips can at times fill miles of California valleys with its colorful blooms.

Identification clues: Thin leaves, sometimes with short lobes; flowers are daisylike, yellow with distinctive white tips. Two other species, *L. fremontii* and *L. chrysanthemoides,* have similarly colored flowers. *L. platyglossa* can be distinguished from them by the short, stiff hairs that cover its leaves, stems, and flower bracts.

Where found: Grasslands; California. Native.

Height: 6–12 inches.   **In bloom:** March–June.

Growing tips: *Light needs* — full sun to part shade; *soil needs* — average organic content, low to average moisture. Can be easily sown from seed in early spring and will flower in about 3 months. Annual.

SUNFLOWERS come in several sizes; the flower-heads of wild species are 2–4 inches across, while those of cultivated species can be up to 1 foot across. Goldfinches, chickadees, and titmice love to eat the nutritious seeds right off the plant. Sunflower seed is also the most favored ingredient in birdseed mixes. The sunflower is the state flower of Kansas.

Identification clues: Tall, with alternate leaves that are broad and pointed at the tip and have rough surfaces; large flower with yellow ray flowers and brown disk flowers.

Where found: Roadsides, fields, waste spaces; throughout the West. Native.

Height: 3–12 feet.   **In bloom:** July–October.

Growing tips: *Light needs* — full sun; *soil needs* — low to rich organic content, low to average moisture. Easy to grow and will tolerate dry, poor soils. Need to replant from seed each year. Annual.

Sunflower — *Helianthus annuus*

Brittlebush —
Encelia farinosa

BRITTLEBUSH is shrublike but seems like a wildflower because of its colorful flowers and low growth. It is included here because it is such a common flowering plant in deserts and is often seen with desert wildflowers. It grows various-size leaves, depending on the amount of moisture it gets — with less moisture, the leaves produced are smaller. A gummy substance from the plant was used as incense by early Spanish Catholics in the area.

Identification clues: Brittle, woody stems with silvery leaves; a single, all-yellow flower tops each flower stalk. The flower is sunflower-like, 1 inch in diameter, and has a yellow center.

Where found: Desert areas or rocky outcroppings; throughout the Southwest. Native.

Height: 1–3 feet.   **In bloom:** November–May.

Growing tips: *Light needs* — full sun; *soil needs* — low to average organic content, low to average moisture. A spectacular winter and early spring blooming plant. Good for covering waste areas with a splash of color. Perennial.

Goldfields — *Lasthenia californica*

GOLDFIELDS can put on a spectacular show of color in California lowlands, where this annual can cover many acres at a time. It is common in grasslands and open woodlands, but will also bloom in deserts if the preceding winter was especially wet. It survives the harsh heat and dryness of the desert summer as seeds.

Identification clues: Leaves thin, opposite, and with sparse hairs; a large area of disk flowers and relatively short ray flowers that are a lighter yellow at their tips and a darker orange-yellow at their bases. Previous species name was *chrysotoma*. Another species, *L. glabrata,* can be found brightening up areas of the California coast with its yellow flowers.

Where found: Grasslands, woodlands, and deserts; from southwest Oregon through California along the coast and in Arizona deserts. Native.

Height: 6–8 inches.   **In bloom:** February–May.

Growing tips: *Light needs* — full sun to part shade; *soil needs* — low to average organic content, low to average moisture. Goldfields is a winter annual that starts blooming in early spring. Sow seeds in fall in the natural range of the plant; in colder areas, sow in spring. Will self-seed in natural range. Annual.

DESERT MARIGOLD adds a bright splash of color along desert roadsides. Its small leaves, covered with fine, woolly hairs, are adaptations to reduce evaporation and make it tolerant of dry conditions. It is sometimes cultivated and available at garden centers.

Identification clues: Small, round-lobed leaves at the base; flowers top long, silvery stalks. The white flowers are daisylike with numerous (25–50) ray flowers and a yellow center. *B. pleniradiata* is similar but grows in southern California deserts; *B. multiradiata* grows in other southwest deserts.

Where found: Roadsides and rocky or sandy dry soils; desert areas of the Southwest. Native.

Height: 6–24 inches.   **In bloom:** March–November; all year in areas with some rain runoff.

Growing tips: *Light needs* — full sun; *soil needs* — low to average organic content, low to average moisture. Does best in garden situations where the soil is sandy. It forms rounded clusters and can be lovely in rock gardens due to its long blooming period. It is a short-lived perennial in the wild and may need to be started from seed each year in the garden. Perennial.

Desert marigold — *Baileya multiradiata*

Sulphur flower — *Eriogonum umbellatum*

SULPHUR FLOWER is one of the 150 species of *Eriogonums* native to North America. It is a member of the buckwheat family and is sometimes called sulphur-flowered buckwheat. *Eriogonums* are common throughout the West and have adapted to a wide variety of habitats, from alpine to desert to coastal areas. This species is often good for rock gardens, for it forms lovely cushions of leaves that gradually grow larger.

Identification clues: Oval basal leaves are gray-green; flower stalks are leafless to the point where they branch, and then they lead to clusters of tiny, yellow flowers. Several leaflike bracts occur where flower stalk branches. *Eriogonums* have similar basal leaves, branching flower stalk, and tiny flowers.

Where found: From desert areas to alpine locations; from southern British Columbia south to southern California and western Colorado. Native.

Height: 6–12 inches.   **In bloom:** April–June.

Growing tips: *Light needs* — full sun; *soil needs* — low to average organic content, low to average moisture. Best grown from seed, since it can be hard to transplant. Plant seeds in late summer to early fall and cover over lightly with soil. Perennial.

Desert zinnia — *Zinnia grandiflora*

DESERT ZINNIA is a common desert plant in the southern Plains states and the Southwest. Its few ray flowers, which look like petals, remain on the plant after pollination and actually help disperse on the wind the seeds that develop from these flowers. Seeds from the disk flowers just fall to the ground. The genus is named after Johann Zinn, who led botanical expeditions in Mexico in the early 1700s.

Identification clues: Leaves are 1 inch long, thin with 3 veins, sometimes slightly curled; flowers are yellow, with 3–6 rounded ray flowers and numerous disk flowers.

Where found: Sparse woodlands and dry desert soils; from Kansas to Nevada south through Texas, New Mexico, and Arizona. Native.

Height: 4–12 inches.

In bloom: May–October.

Growing tips: *Light needs* — full sun; *soil needs* — low to average organic content, low to average moisture. Good for cultivating in desert areas, for it is very drought-tolerant and has a long blooming period. Also good in rock gardens or as a border to other flower beds. Perennial.

LANCE-LEAF STONECROP is just one of the many species of *Sedum* that can be found in the West. Sedums have fleshy leaves with a waxy coating and generally grow close to the ground. All of these features help them conserve water and enable them to grow in sunny, rocky places, where many other plants cannot survive. The common name of stonecrop comes from this habit.

Identification clues: Basal rosettes of small, cylindrical leaves and similar leaves on the flower stalk; flowers are yellow and have 5 sharp-pointed petals. *S. stenopetalum*, narrow-petaled sedum, is similar, but its leaves have a distinct ridge along their lower surface.

Where found: Open, rocky areas; from Washington to California and also in northern Rocky Mountains. Native.

Height: 2–8 inches.

In bloom: June–August.

Growing tips: *Light needs* — full sun; *soil needs* — average organic content, average moisture. Works well in rock gardens and is a drought-tolerant species. Divide in spring or fall for more plants. Perennial.

Lance-leaf stonecrop — *Sedum lanceolatum*

Goldenrod —
Solidago spp.

GOLDENRODS are late-season plants perfect for a wildflower meadow. They attract a myriad of insects, which come to feed on the abundant pollen and nectar. The pollen from goldenrod does not cause hay fever, as is commonly believed, since it is sticky and is rarely airborne.

Identification clues: Many species of goldenrods exist, and they are not easy to distinguish. All have strong, tall stems with bright yellow flowers clustered at the tips. Flowers tend to be arranged along the tops of the branches off the main stem.

Where found: Meadows, fields, roadsides; from Canada south. Native.

Height: 1–5 feet.   **In bloom:** July–October.

Growing tips: *Light needs* — full sun; *soil needs* — low to rich organic content, average moisture. Goldenrods are tough plants that live in moist or dry situations and are lovely in wildflower meadows. They form a dense clump, which can be divided. Will self-seed. Perennial.

Giant evening primrose —
Oenothera hookeri

GIANT EVENING PRIMROSE is named for its large flowers, which first open in the evening, remain open all night, and generally fade during the next day. This habit is designed to attract hawk moths, large moths that hover in front of the flowers while they gather nectar and inadvertently pollinate the flowers. The moths are nocturnal and are attracted to the scent of the flowers as well as their color, which shows well at night.

Identification clues: Lancelike leaves on a straight, stout stalk; flowers are bright yellow, have 4 petals, and are 2–4 inches across. They bloom a few at a time along the tip of the stalk. Many other species of eve-ning primroses also look similar, but they have flowers only half this large.

Where found: Moist, open areas, streamsides, springs; from southern Oregon to southwestern Kan-sas south to Mexico. Native.

Height: 1–5 feet.　　**In bloom:** June–October.

Growing tips: *Light needs* — full sun; *soil needs* — average organic content, average moisture. Giant eve-ning primrose is a rosette of leaves the first year and, in the second year, produces a flowering stalk and then dies. Sow seeds in 2 successive years for potential blooming each year. Biennial.

DOGTOOTH VIOLET is sometimes called "glacier lily" because it is one of the first flowers to bloom as the snowcover melts and recedes. In some instances, a whole area may be covered with these graceful plants. It is not a violet at all, but a beautiful member of the lily family. The bulbs at the base of the plants have in the past been used by Native Americans for food. Wildlife such as bears eat the bulbs, and deer and elk may eat the green seedpods.

Identification clues: Two 4- to 6-inch, shiny, pointed leaves at the base of the plant; flower stalk is leafless, with 1–2 yellow, nodding flowers. Flowers have 3 petals and 3 sepals, all curved back.

Where found: In wet meadows, moist, rich woods, and streamsides; from British Columbia to Eastern Montana south to northern California and northern New Mexico. Native.

Height: 6–12 inches. **In bloom:** March–July.

Growing tips: *Light needs* — part shade to full sun; *soil needs* — rich organic content, average to high moisture. Dogtooth violet needs moist but well-drained soil, so be sure the soil is a little more granular in texture than normal. It also prefers slightly acidic soil with a pH 5 to 6.5. Dogtooth violet takes 3–5 years to grow a flowering plant from seed, and because of this, it is rarely grown by nurseries. Instead, it is usually collected from the wild. Therefore, you should avoid buying this plant from nurseries unless you can be *sure* that they propagated it. Otherwise, just enjoy it in the wild. Perennial.

Dogtooth violet — *Erythronium grandiflorum*

Black-eyed Susan — *Rudbeckia hirta*

BLACK-EYED SUSAN is native to the prairies but moved east and west when settlers made roads to and from the Midwest, for the roadsides became sunny openings in the woods in which the plants could grow. It is named for a famous Swedish botanist, Olaf Rudbeck. The plant is sometimes used to make a yellowish dye.

Identification clues: Short hairs on leaves and stem, leaves lancelike; flowers with long, yellow ray flowers and a rounded, brown center of disk flowers. Cutleaf coneflower, *R. lanciniata*, has a similar flower but deeply lobed leaves; California coneflower, *R. californica*, is similar to black-eyed Susan, except its disk flowers form a tall cone; and western coneflower, *R. occidentalis*, has a large cone of dark disk flowers and no ray flowers.

Where found: Fields, roadsides, waste spaces; from Canada south through Texas. Native.

Height: 2–3 feet. **In bloom:** May–October.

Growing tips: *Light needs* — full sun; *soil needs* — low to rich organic content, average moisture. Can be grown from seed and will start blooming in its second year. Will bloom for 1–3 years and then may need to be replaced. Short-lived perennial.

Buckhorn cholla —
Opuntia acanthocarpa

BUCKHORN CHOLLA grows in such a way as to look a little like deer horns; and, from a distance, the thorns can resemble the velvety covering of a buck's newly grown horns. When bees land on the flowers, the blooms close slightly, ensuring that the bee is dusted with pollen to take to the next bloom.

Identification clues: Branches of this cactus are narrow cylinders, and their straw-colored spines appear in groups of 10–12; flowers are yellow, orange, red, or purple.

Where found: Dry open areas, arid canyons; Arizona, southern California, Colorado. Native.

Height: 3–7 feet.   **In bloom:** April–June.

Growing tips: *Light needs* — full sun; *soil needs* — low organic content, low moisture. Plant in well-drained, sandy soil. Do not overwater. Perennial.

PRICKLY PEAR CACTUS belongs to the genus *Opuntia,* in which those species with cylindrical branching are called chollas and those with flattened branching are called prickly pears. Their fruits can be used to make a delicious jelly as well as other sweets.

Identification clues: Flat, spatula-like sections joined together; 5–11 spines in each cluster, surrounded at their base by little woolly hairs; flowers are yellow.

Where found: Dry plains; from British Columbia to Alberta south to Arizona and Texas. Native.

Height: 3–12 inches.

In bloom: April–July.

Growing tips: *Light needs* — full sun; *soil needs* — low organic content, low moisture. Plant in well-drained, sandy soil. Do not overwater. Perennial.

Prickly pear cactus — *Opuntia polyacantha*

Yellow skunk cabbage — *Lysichitum americanum*

YELLOW SKUNK CABBAGE is a spectacular plant of northwestern swamps. Although it is related to the eastern skunk cabbage — both are in the Arum family — it does not have the same skunky odor to its leaves. It probably got its common name from its similar appearance to the eastern plant. Both plants start sending up leaves while snow is still on the ground.

Identification clues: Very large leaves, 1–5 feet long; yellow, spikelike flower is partially enclosed in a bright yellow hood called a spathe. Not likely to be confused with any other plant.

Where found: Swamps and wet woods; from coastal northern California to southern Alaska east to western Montana. Native.

Height: 1–2½ feet.   **In bloom:** April–July.

Growing tips: *Light needs* — part shade to full shade; *soil needs* — rich organic content, high moisture. A great plant for a wetland or swampy area where you would like some color and the plant's large leaf forms. Should be planted as seedlings. Perennial.

Wood lily —
Lilium philadelphicum

WOOD LILIES are a favorite of wildflower enthusiasts everywhere. They are not very common in the woods and, when found, are almost shocking in their beauty and size. Wood lilies are sometimes pollinated by tiger swallowtail butterflies, which get pollen on the tips of their wings when reaching down to get the nectar.

Identification clues: Unlike most other wild lilies, the wood lily's blossom faces straight up; it is orange with dark spots.

Where found: Moist meadows and woodland clearings; in Rocky Mountains, mostly in eastern portions. Native.

Height: 1–3 feet.   **In bloom:** June–July.

Growing tips: *Light needs* — part shade; *soil needs* — rich organic content, average moisture. Bulbs should be planted 4–5 inches deep in spring or fall. Can be propagated in late summer by dividing the smaller bulbs off the main bulb. This species is becoming rare in the wild and should be protected wherever it is growing. Perennial.

Leopard lily —
Lilium pardalinum

LEOPARD LILY is a favorite of wildflower gardeners because it is amenable to a wide range of climates. It also has large, beautiful flowers. Many varieties have been cultivated and are available at nurseries. Some are of medium height and have a few yellow flowers, while others are tall and have up to 30 flowers.

Identification clues: Lance-shape leaves 4–6 inches long; orange flowers with petals and sepals strongly curved back and covered on the interior of the bloom with maroon and dark red spots.

Where found: Moist, open woods or along streams; from western Oregon into northern California. Native.

Height: 3–8 feet.   **In bloom:** May–July.

Growing tips: *Light needs* — part shade; *soil needs* — average to rich organic content, high moisture. Easy to grow in a woodland wildflower garden or in a partly shaded section of a perennial border. Easily spreads by producing many new bulbs each year. Perennial.

California poppy — *Eschscholtzia californica*

CALIFORNIA POPPY is the state flower of California and rightly so, for it is there that this flower can cover the landscape with literally miles of yellow-orange bloom. The flowers close up at night to protect their pollen from nighttime moisture and then open again at dawn. The seemingly unpronounceable genus name was given in honor of Johann Friedrich Eschscholtz, a botanist who explored the Northwest in the early 1800s.

Identification clues: Blue-green fernlike leaves; 4 bright, yellow-orange petals at tips of stems. Flowers are poppylike and 1–3 inches across. Mexican gold poppy, *E. mexicana,* is a similar species occasionally seen in western Texas and adjoining areas.

Where found: Fields; from Oregon south to southern California, Arizona, and New Mexico. Native.

Height: 6–24 inches.   **In bloom:** February–November.

Growing tips: *Light needs* — full sun; *soil needs* — low to average organic content, low to average moisture. Can be best grown from seed. Plant in fall in warmer climates for early spring bloom; in colder climates, plant in early spring. Annual.

MARIPOSA LILY'S genus name, *Calochortus,* means "beautiful grass" and probably refers to the attractive, grasslike leaves of the plant. *Mariposa* is Spanish for "butterfly" and probably is a reference to the large, lovely petals, which look a little like the wings of sulphur butterflies.

Identification clues: Short plant with grasslike leaves; yellow to bright orange 3-petaled flowers. The very center of the flower is a dark red-brown. When the plant is under shrubs, the flower stalk elongates to bring the flower into the light.

Where found: Desert areas; Southwest states and southern Rocky Mountains. Native.

Height: 6–20 inches.   **In bloom:** March–June.

Growing tips: *Light needs* — full sun; *soil needs* — low to average organic content, low to average moisture. These plants can be difficult to grow in the garden. Some species, not including this one, are also rare and, as with all wild plants, should not be collected from the wild. Perennial.

Mariposa lily — *Calochortus kennedyi*

Blazing star —
Mentzelia lindleyi

BLAZING STARS' flowers first open in the evening and close the next morning. They also bloom in early spring, whereas most others in the genus bloom from early summer to fall. They are a beautiful annual to grow in places where other plants struggle, such as in dry earth with low organic content. The name blazing star is also applied to several species of *Liatris,* but no relationship exists between the two.

Identification clues: Long, narrow leaves with toothed lobes, similar to those of dandelions; flowers are 2–3 inches across, with 5 yellow petals and numerous long stamens.

Where found: Open, sunny, fairly dry areas; in foothills of the Sierra Nevada and along coastal foothills in mid-California. Native.

Height: 6–24 inches. **In bloom:** March–June.

Growing tips: *Light needs* — full sun; *soil needs* — low to rich organic content, low to average moisture. This plant is amenable to a variety of soil conditions so long as it is well-drained. It needs some moisture until it flowers and should be planted from seed in the early spring. Will self-sow. Annual.

Butterfly weed — *Asclepias tuberosa*

BUTTERFLY WEED is one of the best flowers for attracting adult butterflies, which cannot resist the large amounts of nectar in this plant's lovely orange blossoms. Look for little bags of pollen — the plant's means of pollination — stuck to the feet of butterflies and other insects that visit the flowers.

Identification clues: Long narrow, hairy leaves; clusters of bright orange flowers at the tips of stems. Flowers are sometimes red or yellow. Milky juice, found in the stems of other species of milkweed, is not present in butterfly weed.

Where found: Sandy areas, dry fields, roadsides; found throughout the Southwest. Native.

Height: 1–3 feet.   **In bloom:** June–September.

Growing tips: *Light needs* — full sun to part shade; *soil needs* — low to average organic content, low to average moisture. The soil must be well-drained; otherwise, the roots will rot or be attacked by a mold. Once it is established, leave it alone and just enjoy it. Perennial.

DOUGLAS' WALLFLOWER is just one of the many wildflowers that are common throughout the West. Wallflowers are members of the mustard family, called *Cruciferae* because the 4 petals on their flowers form a cross. The flowers of most species in the mustard family are tiny, but those of the wallflowers are among the largest, measuring up to ½ inch across.

Identification clues: Lance-shape leaves with teeth on margins widely spaced; flowers are large, 4-petaled, bright orange-yellow, and clustered atop the stem. Thin seed pods up to 4 inches long develop after flowers fade. Many other species of wallflower exist, and most have similar flowers and seedpods.

Where found: Open, dry flats and rocky slopes; from southwestern Canada south to California and Texas. Native.

Height: 1–3 feet.   **In bloom:** February–September.

Growing tips: *Light needs* — full sun; *soil needs* — low to average organic content, low to average moisture. Can be started from seed in fall. Wallflowers are good for a water-conserving garden. Biennial or perennial.

Douglas' wallflower — *Erysimum capitatum*

Desert mallow — *Sphaeralcea ambigua*

DESERT MALLOW is often found growing in desert areas of the Southwest but can also be found growing around springs, showing what an adaptable plant it is. In its natural habitat, desert mallow can grow up to as many as 100 stems all from a single root. Sometimes it is found with different flower colors, such as white, red, or purple.

Identification clues: Leaves densely covered with silvery hairs, 3 main lobes with wavy edges; flowers are orange and 1–1½ inches across on tall stalks.

Where found: From desert areas to streambanks; from southern Nevada to southern California and southwest Arizona. Native.

Height: 1½–4 feet.   **In bloom:** At lower elevations, any month of the year.

Growing tips: *Light needs* — full sun; *soil needs* — low to average organic content, low to average moisture. Perennial.

Blanketflower — *Gaillardia aristata*

BLANKETFLOWER is extremely tolerant of dry soil conditions and, thus, is ideally suited to today's gardening styles, which put a premium on conserving water. Blanketflowers bloom throughout summer and, when grown in your garden, make good cut flowers that last longer if cut before the blooms fully open. Several annual species such as *G. amblyodon, G. pulchella,* and the perennial *G. pinnatifida* create wonderful shows of bloom in the Southwest and Texas.

Identification clues: Large, daisylike flower with a center of reddish disk flowers and ray flowers that are red near the center and yellow at the tips.

Where found: Plains, prairies, dry hillsides; from Canada to northern Arizona and New Mexico; other species farther south. Native.

Height: 8–24 inches.   **In bloom:** May–September.

Growing tips: *Light needs* — full sun; *soil needs* — average organic content, low to average moisture. Divide in spring every 2–3 years to keep plants vigorous and increase your stock. Perennial.

WILD GINGER is also called long-tailed ginger because of the long, thin tips of its petals. The species name, *caudatum,* means "tail." Members of this genus have a pungent, gingery odor that comes from their crushed leaves or scratched roots, but they are not related to the Asian species of ginger (*Zingiber officinale*), from which we get our cooking spice.

Identification clues: Large, shiny, heart-shape leaves and small hairs along stems and lower leaf veins; flower is attached to leaf axils, is purple-brown, and in this species, has long tapering tails off the tip of each petal. Other species similar but lack tails on petals.

Where found: Moist, rich woods; from British Columbia south along coastal ranges to central California. Native.

Height: 6–12 inches.   **In bloom:** May–July.

Growing tips: *Light needs* — part shade to shade; *soil needs* — rich organic content, average moisture. Wild ginger spreads rhizomes and makes a great ground cover for shady areas. In warmer regions, it remains green all year. Can be divided in fall. Perennial.

Wild ginger — *Asarum caudatum*

CARDINAL FLOWER is one of the favorite flowers of hummingbirds. It is the one flower in our yard that hummingbirds actually fight over. Although most individual hummingbirds extract nectar from the front of the flower, some reach the nectar by poking a hole through the base of the blossom.

Identification clues: Alternate, lance-shape leaves along a single stem; deep red, tubular flowers along the tip of the stem.

Where found: Alongside rivers and streams and in wet meadows; from southern California to Texas. Native.

Height: 2–4 feet.

In bloom: July–October.

Growing tips: *Light needs* — full sun to part shade; *soil needs* — average organic content, high moisture. Grow in a moist area of your property that gets about a half a day of sun. Rhizomes produce offshoot rosettes in fall, and these can be separated and planted elsewhere to increase your stock. Self-seeds in moist conditions. Perennial.

Cardinal flower — *Lobelia cardinalis*

Indian pink — *Silene californica*

INDIAN PINK is another good plant for attracting hummingbirds. Its species name is appropriate since its natural range is almost entirely within the state of California.

Identification clues: Leaves opposite and along with stem are covered with tiny, sticky hairs; flowers are bright red, with 5 deeply notched petals.

Where found: Open woodlands; from southern Oregon to southern California. Native.

Height: 6–20 inches.　**In bloom:** March–July.

Growing tips: *Light needs* — part shade; *soil needs* — average organic content, average moisture. This plant can be grown from seed and will then flower in its second year. Perennial.

Scarlet columbine —
Aquilegia formosa

SCARLET COLUMBINE has red spurs and sepals, an adaptation for hummingbirds, for they favor red flowers. The flowers hang downward, which is also an adaptation for hummingbirds, since these visitors can hover beneath the flower while getting nectar; butterflies and bees need to land in order to sip nectar, and it is difficult for them to do so on the nodding flower of scarlet columbine.

Identification clues: Round-lobed leaves at base and on the stem; bright yellow petals changing to deep red at the backward projecting spurs alternate with the red sepals.

Where found: Rocky slopes, streambanks, woodland clearings as long as they are moist; the Rocky Mountains and Northwest states. Native.

Height: 2–4 feet.   **In bloom:** May–August.

Growing tips: *Light needs* — part shade; *soil needs* — average to rich organic content, average to high moisture. Can be grown from seed and, like other columbines, is a short-lived perennial and may need to be replaced every few years with a younger plant. Perennial.

Desert paintbrush — *Castilleja chromosa*

DESERT PAINTBRUSH is just one of the many species of paintbrush found throughout the West. The genus was named in 1781, in honor of the Spanish botanist Domingo Castillejo. The plants, when in bloom, look like their tips have been dipped in paint, and when massed together, their bright red, orange, and yellow colors are like colorful brush strokes in the landscape. Wyoming paintbrush, *C. linariaefolia,* is the state flower of Wyoming.

Identification clues: Paintbrushes are hard to identify as to species, since they freely hybridize. But as a genus, they are easy to identify. All members have distinctive leafy bracts at the top of the stems that range in color from bright red, as in this species, to orange to yellow to pink.

Where found: Wyoming paintbrush grows in dry woods and sagebrush plains; various species of paintbrush can be found in many different habitats; throughout the West. Native.

Height: 2–5 feet.   **In bloom:** May–September.

Growing tips: *Light needs* — part shade to full sun; *soil needs* — average organic content, average moisture. Paintbrushes are semiparasitic, for when their roots contact those of certain other plants, they attach themselves and absorb some of their nutrients. Because of this, it is difficult to transplant them to the garden. Some species can be grown from seed in the garden. Some species are annual, but this and most others are perennial.

Scarlet gilia — *Ipomopsis aggregata*

SCARLET GILIA is a good flower for attracting hummingbirds, for its long, red, tubed flowers reserve their nectar for these birds since other other visitors cannot reach in that far. As the hummingbirds hover in front of the flowers, they get pollen on their faces, and this is then transferred to the next flower, thus pollinating the plants.

Identification clues: In first year, just a small rosette of leaves; in second year, it has fernlike leaves along the flower stalk. Long, red to pink, tubular flowers almost 2 inches long line one side of the upper stem. Some other desert species of *Ipomopsis* are blue.

Where found: Open meadows, dry hillsides, rocky areas, pine forests; from British Columbia to Montana south to California and New Mexico. Native.

Height: 1–2½ feet.   **In bloom:** May–August.

Growing tips: *Light needs* — full sun; *soil needs* — average organic content, average moisture. A stunning garden flower. Grows rosettes of leaves the first year and a flower stalk the second year. Will readily self-seed. Biennial.

SCARLET MONKEY FLOWER is a good addition to any garden designed to attract hummingbirds. Its bright red flowers call attention to the nectar, protected from insect visitors by flower tubes that are too long for their mouthparts. Many species of *Mimulus* flourish in the West, a number with pink flowers and some with yellow flowers.

Identification clues: Leaves opposite, ovate, toothed along their margins, and slightly ridged between their parallel veins; flowers are deep red with 3 petals bending down and 2 petals standing upright.

Where found: Along streams, springs, moist seeping areas; from the Southwest to Utah and southern Oregon. Native.

Height: 1–3 feet.

In bloom: April–October.

Growing tips: *Light needs* — part shade; *soil needs* — average to rich organic content, high moisture. Perennial.

Scarlet monkey flower — *Mimulus cardinalis*

Firecracker penstemon —
Penstemon eatonii

FIRECRACKER PENSTEMON is a favorite of many hummingbirds that fly through the Southwest on their northward migration in late winter and spring. The long, red tubes and horizontal orientation of penstemon flowers are a good sign of a hummingbird plant. Other insects have trouble landing on the flower, and even if they do, they often cannot reach down the long tube to the nectar.

Identification clues: Leaves opposite, long, and triangular and with wavy margins; flowers are bright red, tubular, and with petal tips not flaring at flower opening but remaining straight. Many other red penstemons exist in the West, but they all have flaring petals at the flower opening.

Where found: Rocky slopes in dry areas; from eastern Nevada to western Utah south to southern California and northwestern Arizona. Native.

Height: 1–3 feet.   **In bloom:** February–July.

Growing tips: *Light needs* — full sun; *soil needs* — low to average organic content, low to average moisture. With added moisture, this species will bloom longer, but soil must be well-drained, with no standing water. Perennial.

Baby blue-eyes — *Nemophila menziesii*

BABY BLUE-EYES is a charming little annual that does very well in garden beds in cooler areas of the country. The genus name means "grove loving," which may refer to its comfort in partly shaded areas. Nurseries have created many varieties, including "alba," which is white, and "grandiflora," which has large flowers.

Identification clues: Small, pinnate leaves; flowers have 5 petals and are blue with white centers.

Where found: Moist, open areas; from southern Oregon through California. Native.

Height: 4–12 inches.   **In bloom:** March–July

Growing tips: *Light needs* — part shade to shade; *soil needs* — average organic content, average moisture. Sow seeds in spring or fall; they will bloom about 3 months after sprouting. Annual.

MOUNTAIN BLUEBELLS can form large groups and are a favorite of many animals, including deer, elk, marmots, and pikas. The genus is named for a famous German botanist, Franz Karl Mertens, who lived from 1764 to 1831.

Identification clues: Leaves are oblong and attached directly to stem with no petiole; flowers are blue, bell-like, and hang down in clusters from the tips of the stems. Another similar species, *M. paniculata*, is more common in the northern Rocky Mountains. Its leaves are attached to the stem with a long petiole.

Where found: Moist areas such as wet meadows and along streambanks; from Montana to Oregon south to New Mexico and central California. Native.

Height: 2–3 feet.   **In bloom:** May–August.

Growing tips: *Light needs* — full sun to part shade; *soil needs* — average to rich organic content, average to high moisture. An easy plant to grow if you have adequate moisture. Will spread by rhizomes. Perennial.

Mountain bluebells — *Mertensia ciliata*

PASQUEFLOWER is the state flower of South Dakota and it blooms just as the snow recedes, which may be as early as March or as late as July, depending on the elevation. The seeds grow feathery filaments while the flower stem continues to get longer; both of these features may help disperse the seeds on the wind. *Anemone* is Greek for "wind" and *pasque* refers to the Paschal, or Easter season, when people often notice this plant in bloom.

Identification clues: Short stalks and much-divided leaves all covered with silky hairs; a single bloom atop each stalk has white to blue-purple flowers, each with 5–8 petal-like sepals and lots of bright yellow pollen in the center. Western pasqueflower, *Anemone occidentalis,* is similar and grows in the Pacific states.

Where found: Streambanks, moist meadows, open woods; from Alaska into Washington down through the Rocky Mountains and the Plains states to northwest Texas. Native.

Height: 6–16 inches.   **In bloom:** March–June.

Growing tips: *Light needs* — part shade to full sun; *soil needs* — average organic content, average to high moisture. Pasqueflower particularly needs moisture when blooming and after that can tolerate dry conditions. Large plants can be divided in early spring. Perennial.

Pasqueflower — *Anemone patens*

Larkspur — *Delphinium nuttallianum*

LARKSPUR is so named because of the spur that projects behind the flower — it is like the hind toe of a lark's foot. This spur contains nectar for the insects that come to the flower and inadvertently pollinate it. Larkspur contains toxic alkaloids that can be harmful to grazing wildlife and livestock, especially before blooming. After blooming, elk are known to feed on them without harmful effects.

Identification clues: Jagged, deeply divided leaves; flowers are blue with a distinctive single spur extending back. Many species of larkspur grow in a variety of habitats.

Where found: Plains and dry ridges; from South Dakota to Wyoming south to northern Southwest. Native.

Height: 6–24 inches.   **In bloom:** March–July.

Growing tips: *Light needs* — part shade to full sun; *soil needs* — average to rich organic content, average moisture. You can sow many species of larkspur in your garden; visit your local native plant society to find out which ones are available and are not collected from the wild. They can be sown from seed in the spring or fall. Perennial.

Colorado columbine — *Aquilegia caerulea*

COLORADO **COLUMBINE** was made the state flower of Colorado in 1899. From that time on, people collected the flowers so much that this species became scarce. In 1925, a law was passed protecting Colorado columbine, and now populations of the plant are recovering; but greater public awareness of plant conservation is still needed to preserve all wild plants.

Identification clues: Round-lobed basal leaves in groups of 3; flower has 5 white petals surrounded by 5 blue-purple sepals. Each petal has a spur (thin tube) projecting out the back, where nectar is stored for pollinators. Flowers are paler in the Northwest.

Where found: Damp, open woods of pines and aspens; throughout the Rocky Mountain states and into northern Arizona and New Mexico. Native.

Height: 1–3 feet.   **In bloom:** June–August.

Growing tips: *Light needs* — part shade to full sun; *soil needs* — rich organic content, average to high moisture. A lovely plant for gardens; it grows easily from seed and may start blooming in its first year. Like many columbines, it can die back after a few years and need to be replaced. Fortunately, it self-seeds. Perennial.

BLUE **VIOLET,** also called western dog violet, is one of the most common violets in the Rocky Mountains. Two types of flowers appear on violets: those that open and those that stay closed. Both develop seeds, but the flowers that remain closed pollinate themselves. As they dry, violet seed capsules create pressure on the seeds, which eventually shoot out and start more plants a few feet away.

Identification clues: Rounded leaves with long petioles and 2 pointed bracts where each petiole joins the stem; flowers are blue to violet.

Where found: Moist woods and meadows; from Alaska south to northern New Mexico and Arizona. Native.

Height: 2–8 inches.   **In bloom:** March–August.

Growing tips: *Light needs* — full sun to part shade; *soil needs* — average to rich organic content, average to high moisture. A lovely little plant that will self-seed. Perennial.

Blue violet — *Viola adunca*

WASHINGTON LUPINE is one of the many perennial species of lupines in the West. Different species of lupines are often difficult to distinguish because they freely hybridize with each other. In the early 1800s, this species was introduced in Europe and became a favorite garden plant thereafter.

Identification clues: Large, palmate leaves, each with 9–16 leaflets that are wide and pointed at the tip; pealike flowers are on spikes and can be blue, white, reddish, yellow, or purple.

Where found: Meadows and moist, open woods; from the southern coast of Alaska down to northern California and farther south in the Sierra Nevada. Native.

Height: 2–5 feet. **In bloom:** May–August.

Growing tips: *Light needs* — full sun to part shade; *soil needs* — average organic content, average moisture. Lupines have a deep taproot, which makes them hard to transplant successfully, so either buy them as small plants or sow by seed. Perennial.

Washington lupine —
Lupinus polyphyllus

Bluebonnet — *Lupinus texensis*

BLUEBONNETS and other lupines are the state flower of Texas, and it is no wonder since they put on one of the best wildflower displays to be seen in spring. The genus name is from the Latin word for "wolf" because these plants were thought to remove nutrients from the soil. In fact, it is just the opposite: the plants grow well in poor soil and have the ability to take nitrogen from the air and make it available to other plants in the soil, so bluebonnets actually enrich the soil.

Identification clues: Two species are called bluebonnets: *L. texensis* and *L. subcarnosus*. Both are low, branching plants with palmate leaves. The leaflets of *L. subcarnosus* are rounded, while those of *L. texensis* are pointed. Both species have blue, pealike flowers on a tall spike. Flower buds of *L. texensis* are conspicuously white, while those of *L. subcarnosus* are blue.

Where found: Sandy soils of rangelands, pastures, woods' edges, and hills; often planted along roadsides; throughout most of Texas except far northwestern and western regions of the state. Native.

Height: 4–16 inches. **In bloom:** March–May.

Growing tips: *Light needs* — full sun; *soil needs* — low to average organic content, low to average moisture. These species are both annuals and need to be sown from seed. Once established, they can self-sow. Annual.

Harebell — *Campanula rotundifolia*

HAREBELLS are adapted to grow in a variety of conditions, from alpine meadows and rocky cliffs to low-lying prairies. In alpine environments, harebells remain short — 4 to 6 inches tall — and the leaves are short and hairy to conserve moisture. In richer, warmer environments, the plants are taller and the leaves longer. Harebell is a wild relative of the garden species called bellflowers.

Identification clues: Extremely narrow leaves and a thin wiry stem; topped by light blue, bell-like flowers in which the petals are fused together.

Where found: From alpine meadows to prairies; throughout the West. Native.

Height: 4–24 inches.   **In bloom:** June–September.

Growing tips: *Light needs* — full sun to part shade; *soil needs* — average organic content, low to average moisture. Plants can be divided in spring when they are still dormant. Perennial.

SKY PILOT is generally found in alpine areas nestled among rocks or on the excavation mounds of pocket gophers. If you happen to step on the plant, you may carry its strong, skunklike odor with you for quite a while. The genus name, *viscosum*, means "sticky" and refers to the stickiness of the stems and leaves, which may deter some nonpollinating insects from getting to the flowers.

Identification clues: Three- to 6-inch-long leaves with whorls of tiny leaflets all along them; cluster of bright blue, 5-petaled flowers at the top of a stalk. Skunky odor of crushed leaves helps to identify this plant.

Where found: Rocky, alpine slopes; throughout the Rocky Mountains, from southern British Columbia and Alberta south to northern Arizona and New Mexico. Native.

Height: 6–16 inches.   **In bloom:** June–August.

Growing tips: *Light needs* — full sun; *soil needs* — average organic content, average moisture. Seeds can be sown in late summer to fall. Perennial.

Sky pilot — *Polemonium viscosum*

Blue penstemon —
Penstemon cyaneus

BLUE PENSTEMON is a gorgeous flower of the northen Rocky Mountains and often can be found growing along with sagebrush. It is also a common roadside plant in open, gravelly areas. When introduced into garden soil, it does beautifully.

Identification clues: Basal leaves lancelike and 6 inches long; leaves farther up the stem are opposite and clasp the stem; flowers are purple at tubular base and blue at tip where petals flare out.

Where found: Dry, gravelly flats and hillsides; Idaho, Montana, and Wyoming. Native.

Height: 1–2½ feet.   **In bloom:** June–August.

Growing tips: *Light needs* — full sun; *soil needs* — low to average organic content, low to average moisture. Perennial.

Blue flax — *Linum perenne*

BLUE FLAX is a lovely, delicate, prairie flower. The blossoms stay open only for the morning and then close for the rest of the day. Its stiff stem shows why its cultivated relative is used to make flax for cloth and linen. This plant is often included in commercial wildflower meadow mixes.

Identification clues: Small leaves close to fine stem; branches droop at tips, where blue, 5-petaled flowers are attached.

Where found: Prairies, plains, dry fields; from Alaska and Canada south through Texas. Native.

Height: 1–2 feet.

In bloom: June–July.

Growing tips: *Light needs* — full sun; *soil needs* — average organic content, low to average moisture. Flax can tolerate dry conditions and, therefore, is perfect for a dry wildflower meadow. Perennial.

MONKSHOOD is named for its uppermost sepal, which looks like the cowl of a monk's robe. All parts of the plant are poisonous to humans and, most likely, to many insects that might otherwise consider eating it. The entrance to the flower is sized just right for bumblebees, who inadvertently get pollen on their bellies and help pollinate this lovely plant.

Identification clues: Distinctive flowers are arranged along a tall spike. They are generally blue-purple, although sometimes whitish in the Northwest. The upper petal is like a hood over the lower petals, which are fused together and form a rounded opening.

Where found: Moist, mountain meadows and along streams; throughout mountain ranges from British Columbia to southern New Mexico. Native.

Height: 1½–6 feet.

In bloom: June–September.

Growing tips: *Light needs* — part shade to full sun; *soil needs* — average to rich organic content, average to high moisture. Monkshood produces new tubers at the base of the plant each year, and these can be divided off in spring to increase your stock. Perennial.

Monkshood — *Aconitum columbianum*

DESERT CHIA is in the mint family, as can be seen by its square stem and the tight clusters of flowers that surround the stem. Its seeds have been used as food by Native Americans.

Identification clues: Fernlike leaves are mostly basal; blue flowers occur in tight clusters along tips of stems.

Where found: Desert areas; Arizona. Native.

Height: 6–24 inches.   **In bloom:** March–July.

Growing tips: *Light needs* — full sun; *soil needs* — low to average organic content, low to average moisture. Annual.

Desert chia — *Salvia columbariae*

California bluebell — *Phacelia campanularia*

CALIFORNIA BLUEBELL tends to grow naturally in desert areas but is a very adaptable plant and can also do well in gardens, as the British have known for a long time.

Identification clues: Leaves ovate with irregularly toothed margin; flowers have deep blue, fused petals.

Where found: Open, dry, sandy areas; Southern California. Native.

Height: 6–30 inches.   **In bloom:** February–May.

Growing tips: *Light needs* — full sun; *soil needs* — low organic content, low to average moisture. Sow seed in early spring. Easy to grow; may self-sow. Annual.

Wild hyacinth — *Dichelostemma pulchellum*

WILD HYACINTHS are a member of the lily family, as can be seen by their long, parallel-veined leaves and their flower parts, which are in multiples of 3. They can make nice additions to rock gardens. The corms were collected by Pima and Papago Indians for food.

Identification clues: Thin, grasslike leaves; tight clusters of pale blue-violet flowers top a single, leafless stalk.

Where found: Dry, lowland areas; from the Pacific states to Arizona; also southern Utah and Nevada. Native.

Height: 6–24 inches.   **In bloom:** January–May.

Growing tips: *Light needs* — part shade to full sun; *soil needs* — average organic content, low to average moisture. These plants prefer well-drained soils, which means adding sand to your soil mixture. Like other plants with corms, they will increase in number slowly from year to year. The plant dies back to the ground by midsummer and overwinters as a corm. Perennial.

ROCKY MOUNTAIN IRIS is believed to have been used by Native Americans in two ways. One was to make a green dye, and the other was to use the poisonous roots to make a substance they could put on their arrow tips to more easily kill their prey. The leaves of this iris are avoided by wild and domestic grazing animals, leaving the plant free to spread over large areas and fill them with its beautiful blooms.

Identification clues: Long, swordlike basal leaves; typical iris flower that is blue. This is the only species of iris native to the Rocky Mountain region.

Where found: Wet meadows; from British Columbia and North Dakota to southern California and New Mexico. Native.

Height: 1–3 feet.   **In bloom:** May–July.

Growing tips: *Light needs* — full sun; *soil needs* — average to rich organic content and average to high moisture. Perfect plant for a wet meadow area or streamside. Spreads by rhizomes and is hardy in cold climates. Perennial.

Rocky Mountain iris — *Iris missouriensis*

Douglas' iris — *Iris douglasiana*

DOUGLAS' IRIS is one of the more common irises along the Pacific coast. One of its great advantages is that it starts blooming very early in the year, even in January. The flowers can be a variety of colors, and many hybrids exist since this species regularly cross-pollinates other iris species.

Identification clues: One- to 2-foot-long, sword-shape leaves; flowers vary in color from cream to yellow to lavender to red-purple.

Where found: Moist, grassy hills and open woods along the Pacific coast; from southern Oregon to southern California. Native.

Height: 1–3 feet.   **In bloom:** January–May.

Growing tips: *Light needs* — part shade; *soil needs* — average to rich organic content, average moisture. Does not survive cold winters, so is best grown along the Pacific coast. A good plant for a slightly wetter area of the rock garden. Spreads by rhizomes. Perennial.

Strawberry hedgehog cactus — *Echinocereus engelmannii*

STRAWBERRY HEDGEHOG CACTUSES are low-growing and form clusters up to several feet in diameter. They are named for their stems, which are small and rounded like a hedgehog. The flowers open by day but close each night. They form fruits that are eaten by desert rodents and birds. Another closely related species is claretcup hedgehog, *E. triglochidatus.* This species spreads to higher elevations and is pollinated by hummingbirds, which need to reach way inside its trumpet-shape flowers.

Identification clues: Several cylindrical stems clustered together; each spine cluster has several longer, central spines, some flattened at their base. Flowers are red-purple.

Where found: Desert areas; Southwest. Native.

Height: 6–18 inches.   **In bloom:** February–May.

Growing tips: *Light needs* — full sun; *soil needs* — low to average organic content, low moisture. Need to be placed in sandy, well-drained soils, where their short roots can quickly absorb water. Do not overwater, but also do not neglect. Perennial.

CHECKERBLOOM will look familiar to those who have tried to grow hollyhocks in their gardens, for both are members of the Mallow family. This is a plant often used in gardens and available in nurseries as cultivars called rosey gem and pink beauty.

Identification clues: Basal leaves round with rounded teeth along the edge; leaves on the stem have many lobes; flowers are 1–1½ inches across, with 5 petals that have fine white stripes toward the center.

Where found: Wet, grassy areas; from southern Oregon through California along the coast and slightly inland. Native.

Height: 6–24 inches.   **In bloom:** February–June.

Growing tips: *Light needs* — part shade to full sun; *soil needs* — average organic content, average to high moisture. Lovely plant for the rock garden, the flower stalks forming a vertical element to your garden design. Perennial.

Checkerbloom — *Sidalcea malvaeflora*

STICKY GERANIUM is a common roadside plant in mountainous areas. Its seeds are sprung from the plant with a little catapult mechanism that you can see when the seedheads have dried. Wild geraniums are not directly related to the geraniums normally bought at nurseries, which are members of the genus *Pelargonium*.

Identification clues: Leaves mostly basal and with 5–7 jagged lobes; flowers about 1 inch across, pink to purple with darker veins on each petal. Many other geraniums thrive throughout the West.

Where found: Roadsides, meadows, open woods; from Alberta to British Columbia south to northern California and Colorado. Native.

Height: 1–2 feet.   **In bloom:** May–July.

Growing tips: *Light needs* — full sun to part shade; *soil needs* — average to rich organic content, low to high moisture. This is a very adaptable plant that can spread aggressively by rhizomes. Perennial.

Sticky geranium — *Geranium viscosissimum*

Fairy primrose — *Primula angustifolia*

FAIRY PRIMROSE differs from its cousin Parry primrose in several ways: it is much smaller, it is nestled close to the ground, it grows in drier areas, and it smells sweet instead of rank. Fairy primrose is now grown horticulturally and is a lovely early bloomer for a rock garden.

Identification clues: Very small, smooth leaves close to the ground; flowers are small, 5-petaled, and magenta with yellow centers.

Where found: Among boulders and rocky areas of alpine slopes; from Utah and Colorado to northern New Mexico. Native.

Height: 2–4 inches.   **In bloom:** May–June.

Growing tips: *Light needs* — full sun to part shade; *soil needs* — average organic content, average moisture. Perennial.

REDWOOD SORREL has the charming habit — shared by most other members of the genus — of folding its leaflets down around the stem at night and then opening them up the next morning. The flower also closes at night and may remain closed on cloudy days. As with other members of *Oxalis*, the leaves have a tangy flavor because they contain oxalic acid.

Identification clues: Large, cloverlike leaves with gray marks on the leaflet midveins; flowers are pink or white, with yellow at the base of their 5 petals.

Where found: Under conifers along the coast; from Vancouver to northern California. Native.

Height: 3–4 inches.   **In bloom:** February–September.

Growing tips: *Light needs* — shade; *soil needs* — rich in organic matter, average moisture. A plant best grown in its native haunt, which is along the Northwest coast, where the mild winters and cool summers help it thrive. Spreads by rhizomes; sow seeds in fall. Excellent for shady ground cover. Perennial.

Redwood sorrel — *Oxalis oregana*

Parry primrose —
Primula parryi

PARRY PRIMROSE is one of the most spectacular flowers of the alpine regions, being relatively tall for its alpine habitat and having brilliantly colored flowers. The plant has an unpleasant odor to our noses but may help to attract pollinators. It is named after the botanist Charles Parry, who lived in the West in the late 1800s.

Identification clues: Basal rosette of upright, lance-like leaves 6–10 inches long; cluster of magenta flowers with yellow centers on tall stalk.

Where found: Alpine areas that are wet, such as streambanks, seeps, and bog edges; from Montana to Idaho south down through the Rocky Mountains to New Mexico. Native.

Height: 6–18 inches.   **In bloom:** July–August.

Growing tips: *Light needs* — full sun to part shade; *soil needs* — average to rich organic content, average to high moisture. Perennial.

Desert sand verbena — *Abronia villosa*

DESERT SAND VERBENAS, with sufficient rainfall in late winter, can create spectacular shows in early spring, forming carpets of bloom either alone or with other species of wildflowers. They also can be a fine addition to gardens, for they have nice foliage, fragrant flowers, and help attract butterflies.

Identification clues: A low, trailing plant with ovate leaves; pink to purple flowers with white centers form clusters at the tips of stalks that arise from the trailing stem. The leaves, stems, and outside of the flowers are covered with tiny hairs. A similar species. *A. angustifolia*, grows in the deserts of western Texas.

Where found: Deserts, roadsides, dry streambeds, and other sandy areas; Southern California and western Arizona. Native.

Height: 3–6 inches.　　**In bloom:** February–April.

Growing tips: *Light needs* — full sun; *soil needs* — low to average organic content, low to average moisture. Add sand to the soil, for these plants like well-drained soil. They can be planted from seed from fall to early spring. They make a nice ground cover and will self-seed. Annual.

QUEEN'S CROWN is an alpine member of *Sedum* that lives in wet meadows, streamsides, and bogs. This species, along with the similar king's crown, have foliage that turns bright red in fall. Many sedums are used in cultivation for rock gardens.

Identification clues: Fleshy, spatula-like leaves ½–1 inch long surround the stems; flowers have 5 pointed petals, are pink to reddish, and are clustered into a sphere at the tip of the stem. King's crown, *S. rosea*, is similar, but it is shorter and has 4-petaled flowers grouped in a more flattopped cluster.

Where found: Among rocks of wet meadows or streambanks; from Montana south to Arizona and New Mexico. Native.

Height: 6–12 inches.   **In bloom:** June–September.

Growing tips: *Light needs* — full sun; *soil needs* — average organic content, high moisture. Can be propagated through division in fall or spring. Perennial.

Queen's crown — *Sedum rhodanthum*

Moss campion — *Silene acaulis*

MOSS CAMPION is found in mountains above timberline and grows very slowly, as do most alpine plants, due to the short growing season, the harshness of the climate, and the lack of available nutrients. It may take a moss campion 25 years to grow a foot in diameter. Because of this, we must take care not to hurt these and other plants when hiking through alpine areas.

Identification clues: Small lancelike leaves clustered together in a cushionlike form; flowers are pink, 5 petals each with a little notch at their tip.

Where found: Gravelly areas and talus slopes in alpine region; in mountains from Alaska south to Arizona and New Mexico. Native.

Height: 1–2 inches.

In bloom: July–September.

Growing tips: *Light needs* — full sun; *soil needs* — average organic content, average moisture. Excellent rock garden plant. Spreads slowly. Perennial.

Elephant's-head — *Pedicularis groenlandica*

ELEPHANT'S-HEAD is a common flower of open wet areas in the mountains. It is pollinated primarily by bumblebees, which hold on to the ears of the little "elephants" as they go after the pollen of the flower. Like many plants with flowers arranged on a spike, the individual flowers start blooming from the lowest to the highest, with a few opening each day.

Identification clues: Fernlike leaves; unmistakable flowers are borne on long spikes, and each looks like the tiny head of a pink elephant with its trunk up-turned.

Where found: Wet, mountain meadows, along streams and lakes; from Alaska south to Wyoming and Oregon and then south through the Rocky Mountains and Sierra Nevada. Native.

Height: 1–3 feet.   **In bloom:** June–August.

Growing tips: *Light needs* — full sun; *soil needs* — average to rich in organic content, high moisture. Takes 2–3 years for first blooms if started from seed. Perennial.

OWL'S CLOVER can cover large areas of desert regions, especially following a wet winter. It is sometimes parasitic on neighboring grasses, but this is not a necessity for it to become established.

Identification clues: Thin, feathery leaves; flowers pink to red-purple with a yellow spot of pollen; the tips of the bracts under each flower are also red-purple.

Where found: Low, grassy, and desert areas; from California through southern Arizona. Native.

Height: 4–16 inches.   **In bloom:** March–May

Growing tips: *Light needs* — full sun; *soil needs* — low to average organic content, low moisture. Has a particular need for well-drained soils. Seeds can be sown in fall. Annual.

Owl's clover — *Orthocarpus purpurascens*

Fireweed — *Epilobium angustifolium*

FIREWEED is known for its habit of colonizing burned-over areas or other sites cleared of vegetation, such as ski slopes and power-line right-of-ways. Other reasons for the name may be that masses of its blooms can look like fire, and its tufted seeds resemble smoke as they disperse. Young shoots can be eaten like asparagus, and the plants are grazed by deer and elk.

Identification clues: A tall, leafy stalk; when in the process of blooming, it has buds at the top, 4-petaled flowers in the middle, and long, thin seed pods beginning to develop beneath.

Where found: Clearings and burned areas; throughout the West. Native.

Height: 3–7 feet.　　**In bloom:** June–September.

Growing tips: *Light needs* — full sun; *soil needs* — average organic content, low to average moisture. Can be divided in fall or spring. Perennial.

Fairy slipper — *Calypso bulbosa*

FAIRY SLIPPER is named for the delicate structure of its tiny flower, which resembles a diminutive slipper — one that could fit only a woodland fairy. This plant is often found growing near or on a rotted log, where its roots associate with special fungi that help them absorb nutrients. The genus name, *Calypso*, refers to the beautiful nymph in Homer's *Odyssey*, and *bulbosa* refers to the bulblike corm at the base of the plant.

Identification clues: A single, ovate leaf at the base and a short, leafless stalk; the single flower has 5 pink petal-like structures above a spotted, saclike formation.

Where found: Moist or wet coniferous woods; from Alaska and northern Canada south into California and Arizona. Native.

Height: 6–8 inches. **In bloom:** March–June.

Growing tips: *Light needs* — shade; *soil needs* — rich organic content, average to high moisture. Flower stalk grows in spring; single leaf grows in late summer and overwinters; both die back in early summer after bloom fades. You cannot grow this plant in your garden because it needs special fungi associated with its roots. And you cannot buy it except from sources that have dug it from the wild since no one knows how to propagate it efficiently. So just enjoy this species in the wild. Perennial.

PACIFIC BLEEDING HEART is a lovely plant to grow in a wild garden because of its luxuriant foliage and long period of bloom. Its common name refers to the heart shape of the flower; its genus name means "double center" and refers to the two halves of the "heart"; and the species name means "graceful."

Identification clues: Much divided, fernlike leaves grow from base of plant; pink, heart-shape flowers are borne on separate, leafless stalks. Blossoms are sometimes white. A small version of this genus is called steershead, *D. uniflora.* It is only 4 inches high and 2 of its petals curve out like steer's horns.

Where found: Rich woodlands and by the side of streams; along the coast from central British Columbia to central California coast and mountains. Native.

Height: 1–1½ feet. **In bloom:** March–August.

Growing tips: *Light needs* — part shade to shade; *soil needs* — average to rich organic content, average moisture. This is an easy plant to grow, and many varieties of it are offered at nurseries. Its tubers can be separated in fall or spring to increase your stock. Leaves and flowers die back in late summer. Good in shaded gardens. Perennial.

Pacific bleeding heart — *Dicentra formosa*

Western shooting star —
Dodecatheon pulchellum

WESTERN SHOOTING STAR is aptly named for the form of its beautiful flowers, which look like little comets or fireworks in the air. Their petals are swept back as the flower points down and the anthers and pistil form a point below the petals. Shooting stars are closely related to our common houseplants called cyclamens, which also have reflexed petals. Sometimes shooting stars are also called bird bills.

Identification clues: Narrow leaves only at the base of the plant; flower stalk with several pink to purple flowers with swept-back petals. Several species share these same characteristics. *D. pulchellum* is one of the most widespread.

Where found: Wet meadows and other smaller grassy areas; throughout the West. native.

Height: 6–12 inches.   **In bloom:** June–August.

Growing tips: *Light needs* — part shade to full sun; *soil needs* — average to rich organic content, average to high moisture. After flowering, the leaves and flower stalk die back to the ground, and the plant is dormant from late summer through winter. Perennial.

Glossary

Alternate leaves: Leaves growing singly on alternate sides of the stem.

Anther: The section of the male part of a flower where pollen is produced.

Basal leaves: Leaves near the ground at the base of a plant.

Basal rosette: Compressed whorl of leaves that radiates from a central point at the base of the stem.

Bracts: Small, leaflike appendage on a stem or flower.

Compound leaves: Large leaves composed of many smaller leaflets.

Corm: Underground swollen portion of a stem.

Disk flowers: Clusters of numerous tiny flowers on the central part of a composite family flower, such as the center of an oxeye daisy.

Flowerhead: Grouping of many small flowers into one bunch on the top of a stem.

Leaf axil: Point between the stem and the base of the leaf attachment.

Leaf scar: Small mark left on a plant stem showing the point where a shed leaf was formerly attached.

Opposite leaves: Leaves growing in pairs opposite each other on the stem.

Palmate: In an arrangement like the fingers of a hand.

Petiole: Leaf stem.

Pinnate: Leaflets opposite each other along a leaf stem.

Pistil: The total female reproductive organ in the flower, made up of the egg, ovary, style, and stigma.

Ray flowers: Individual flowers with a long, straplike petal that are usually on the edge of a flowerhead, such as those around the edge of an oxeye daisy.

Reflexed petal: Petal that bends downward.

Rhizome: Underground stem that often grows horizontally and may produce new stems.

Rosette: Compressed whorl of leaves that radiates from a central point above the roots.

Runner: Aboveground stem that, when it touches the ground, may grow roots and possibly a new stem.

Sepal: One of an outer whorl of leaflike structures that enclose the flower at the bud stage.

Spp.: When following a genus name, means various species in that genus.

Stamen: The whole male reproductive organ in the flower, made up of the filament and the anther.

Taproot: Main central root.

Tuber: A swelling on a rhizome that usually stores food.

Resources

Books on Wildflowers

Ajilvsgi, Geyata. 1984. *Wildflowers of Texas.* Fredricksburg, TX: Shearer Publishing.

Arnberger, Leslie P. 1982. *Flowers of the Southwest Mountains.* Tucson, AZ: Southwest Parks and Monuments Association.

Art, Henry W. 1990. *The Wildflower Gardener's Guide: California, Desert Southwest.* Pownal, VT: Storey Communications, Inc.

Craighead, John J., Frank C. Craighead, Jr., and Ray J. Davis. 1963. *A Field Guide to Rocky Mountain Wildflowers.* Boston: Houghton Mifflin Company.

Dannen, Kent and Donna. 1981. *Rocky Mountain Wildflowers.* Estes Park, CO: Tundra Publications.

Dodge, Natt N. 1985. *Flowers of the Southwest Deserts.* Tucson, AZ: Southwest Parks and Monuments Association.

Knopf, Jim. 1991. *The Xeriscape Flower Gardener.* Boulder, CO: Johnson Books.

Martin, Laura C. 1986. *The Wildflower Meadow Book.* Charlotte, NC: East Woods Press.

National Wildflower Research Center. 1989. *Wildflower Handbook.* Austin, TX: Texas Monthly Press.

Niehaus, Theodore F. 1984. *A Field Guide to Southwestern*

and Texas Wildflowers. Boston: Houghton Mifflin Company.

———. 1976. *A Field Guide to Pacific States Wildflowers.* Boston: Houghton Mifflin Company.

Nokes, Jill. 1986. *How to Grow Native Plants of Texas and the Southwest.* Austin, TX: Texas Monthly Press.

Peterson, Roger T., and Margaret McKenny. 1968. *A Field Guide to Wildflowers.* Boston: Houghton Mifflin Company.

Phillips, Harry R. 1985. *Growing and Propagating Wildflowers.* Chapel Hill, NC: University of North Carolina Press.

Sperka, Marie. 1984. *Growing Wildflowers: A Gardener's Guide.* New York: Charles Scribner's Sons.

Stokes, Donald and Lillian. 1985. *A Guide to Enjoying Wildflowers.* Boston: Little, Brown and Company.

Strickler, Dr. Dee. 1990. *Alpine Wildflowers.* Columbia Falls, MT: The Flower Press.

Taylor, Ronald J. 1986. *Rocky Mountain Wildflowers.* Seattle: The Mountaineers.

Wasowski, Sally and Andy. 1988. *Native Texas Plants.* Austin, TX: Texas Monthly Press.

Wilson, Jim. 1992. *Landscaping with Wildflowers.* Boston: Houghton Mifflin Company.

Wildflower Seed Mixes

Absorka Seed. Rt. 1, Box 97, Manderson, WY 82432.

Abundant Life Seed Foundation. P.O. Box 772, Port Townsend, WA 98368.

Alternative Groundcovers, Inc. P.O. Box 49092, Colorado Springs, CO 80919. 719-548-1471.

Applewood Seed Company. 5380 Vivian Street, Arvada, CO 80002. 303-431-6283.

Clyde Robin Seed. P.O. Box 2366, Castro Valley, CA 18974. 415-785-0425.

Dean Swift Seed Company. P.O. Box B, Jaroso, CO 81138.

Granite Seed. P.O. Box 8A, Clovis, NM 88101.

Harris Seeds. P.O. Box 22960, Rochester, NY 14624. 716-442-9386.

High Altitude Gardens. P.O. Box 4619, Ketchum, ID 83340.

Johnny's Selected Seeds. Foss Hill Road, Albion, ME 04910. 207-437-9294.

Larner Seeds. P.O. Box 407, Bolinas, CA 94924-0407.

Little Valley Farm. Rt. 3, Box 544, Spring Green, WI 53581. 608-935-3324.

Lofts Seed, Inc. P.O. Box 146, Bound Brook, NJ 08805. 800-526-3890.

McLaughlin's Seeds. Buttercup's Acre, Mead, WA 99021-0550.

Park Seed Company, Inc. Cokesbury Road, Greenwood, SC 29647. 803-223-7333.

Plants of the Southwest. Rt. 6, Box 11A, Aqua Fria Road, Santa Fe, NM 87501.

S and S Seeds. P.O. Box 1275, Carpinteria, CA 93013.

Vermont Wildflower Farm. Route 7, Charlotte, VT 05445.

W. Atlee Burpee Company. 300 Park Avenue, Warminster, PA 18974. 215-674-4915.

Good Plant Sources

For a list of nurseries that are responsible sellers of native plants, buy the book *Nursery Sources: Native Plants and Wildflowers,* published by the New England Wildflower Society, Hemenway Road, Framingham, MA 01701. 508-877-7630.

Native Plant Societies

Alaska Native Plant Society. P.O. Box 141613, Anchorage, AK 99514.

Arizona Native Plant Society, P.O. Box 41206, Tucson, AZ 85717.

California Native Plant Society. 909 12th Street, Suite 116, Sacramento, CA 95814.

Canadian Wildflower Society. 75 Ternhill Crescent, North York, Ontario, Canada, M1L 3H8.

Colorado Native Plant Society. P.O. Box 200, Fort Collins, CO 80522.

Idaho Native Plant Society. P.O. Box 9451, Boise, ID 83707.

Montana Native Plant Society. P.O. Box 92, Bozeman, MT 59771.

National Wildflower Research Center. 2600 FM 973 North, Austin, TX 78725.

Native Plant Society of New Mexico. 443 Live Oak Loop N.E., Albuquerque, NM 87122.

Native Plant Society of Oregon. 1920 Engel Avenue N.W., Dalem, OR 97304.

Native Plant Society of Texas. P.O. Box 891, Georgetown, TX 78627.

Northern Nevada Native Plant Society. P.O. Box 8965, Reno, NV 89507.

Utah Native Plant Society. 3631 South Carolyn Street, Salt Lake City, UT 84106.

Washington Native Plant Society. Department of Botany KB-15, University of Washington, Seattle, WA 98195. 206-543-1942.

Wyoming Native Plant Society. P.O. Box 1471t, Cheyenne, WY 82003.

Index to the Gallery of Wildflowers